Born in 1941, Olive Senior spent her early years in Trelawny and another rural Jamaican parish, Westmoreland. In her Trelawny village she was one of ten children in a poor family; she was an only child in her relatives' Westmoreland home of comparative wealth. Moving between households, she was 'pretty much being shifted between the two extremes of a continuum based on race, colour and class in Jamaica.'

She began in journalism, working for the *Gleaner* while still a student at Montego Bay High School. She has a degree in print journalism from Carleton University, Ottawa, Canada, and has studied in the United Kingdom as a Thomson Scholar. A former Editor of *Social and Economic Studies* at the University of the West Indies, Olive Senior is Editor of *Jamaica Journal* and Managing Director of Institute of Jamaica Publications Ltd.

She is the author of *The Message is Change* (on the 1972 General Elections in Jamaica), *Talking of Trees* (a collection of poems) and a reference book, *A-Z of Jamaican Heritage*. She has recently completed a book on Women in the Caribbean. *Summer Lightning*, winner of the Commonwealth Writers' Prize for 1987, is Olive Senior's first collection of short stories.

Summer Lightning

and other stories

to SEE I
to strike LIE

Olive Senior

Longman

Longman Caribbean Limited
Trinidad and Jamaica

Longman Group UK Limited,
Longman House,
Burnt Mill, Harlow,
Essex CM20 2JE, England
and Associated Companies
throughout the world.

First published 1986
Eighth impression 1991

Set in Linotron 202

Produced by Longman Group (FE) Ltd
Printed in Hong Kong

ISBN 0 582 78627 4

Contents

Summer Lightning

THE man came to stay with them for a few weeks each year. For his 'nerves' they said. They always gave him the garden room. No one called it by that name but that was how the boy thought about it. This room by some architectural whimsy completely unbalanced the house. There on one side were three large bedrooms and a bathroom, in the middle the kitchen and the dining room and what the uncle called the living room and the aunt the parlour, and on the far side this one bedroom. Adjoining it was the side verandah where the full blue-seam crocus bags of pimento were sometimes stacked, where the uncle sat on Sundays when the travelling barber came to cut his hair, and where visitors who were not up to the standard of the front verandah were received, standing.

The room was the smallest in the house. It had no glass, no mirrors, just a bed, the uncle's desk, and ten green jalousies. In fact most of the house was painted green since the aunt thought it was a restful colour for the eyes. One of the doors led to the dining room, one to the side verandah, and the other down broken marble steps into a tangled and overgrown garden.

It was amazing that a room with so many openings could be so private. But it was. And it was the boy's secret room, a place where he could hide during thunderstorms. "Lightning only strike liard," Brother Justice had told him once, and since then he had lived in an agony of mid-afternoons when sheet lightning washed the house. "Lightning is Jah triple vision. Is like X-ray dat," Bro. Justice also said. "When Jah want to search I out Jah send the lightning to see right through I". Brother Justice also told him that he would be safe from lightning only in a place

1

where there was no glass at all since everybody knew that "glass draw lightning," glass and "shiny instrument". Brother Justice said that that was why he had no mirror in his hut, that and the fact that glass is an instrument of Babylon. Whenever lightning started to flash, Bro. Justice would put into his crocus bag his machete, the only shiny instrument he possessed, for he kept the blade sharp. But then Bro. Justice knew everything, was right about everything, including the lightning.

Thus it came about that at the first sign of rain the boy would go into the garden room, slowly and in a certain order which he had worked out as most satisfying close all ten jalousies, lock the doors, and in darkness to which his eyes soon became accustomed, wait out the storm. No one troubled him for the thunderstorms usually coincided with the aunt and uncle's afternoon rest.

He was never lonely for he harboured many secret places inside him. It was as if when he closed the windows and doors, the doors of his mind flew open one after another, like living inside the heart of an opening flower.

He was enchanted by these places for they were located in another world, occupied different space, transcended dimensions. People and animals changed places at will, and he was the master of them all. Bro. Justice was the only actual living human being he knew who also moved in this world, and Bro. Justice he could never transform into anything but what he was. The aunt and uncle were excluded because he couldn't see them stiff and proper quite fitting into and accepting the mysteries of this world. At first his father and mother sometimes appeared but his memories of them got dimmer and dimmer and finally he saw them only as through the one winking and mysterious green eye in his uncle's box level which swam up and down in a fluid.

And this world was so satisfying that after a time even when there was no sign of rain he would still go into the room cool and shaded for there his uncle kept his desk, a goldmine of pigeonholes. Though he was forbidden to touch, he intimately knew its secrets: semi-precious stones from Panama and Costa

Rica, unpolished lead weights, a small whetstone, and the box level with the green fluid in which reposed the eye, or so it seemed, that winked at him when he tilted it. There were bundles of string and rusty nails forgotten and still in tarpaper. There were oil cans and oil stains and grease and a great many papers tied with string that looked official and held no interest. And as long as he was alone in this room he was happy because he knew instinctively that if in the world he had nothing else, he was still rich because he had this space which allowed him to explore secret places inside him.

The old man had been coming for years; the boy was the newcomer to the house, the room had been 'his' for a short time only. At first he did not mind the man coming and occupying the room for he brought a welcome chaos to a too-ordered household. The boy thought he was, in a funny kind of way, nice, though his smile was crooked and at times his eyes glazed over and his mouth trembled and he mumbled to himself. He also did not appear to see too well and this the boy liked, for he could hide in the shadows and listen to the man's mumblings. The man also brought him presents. One was a tiny elephant carved in ivory. The man told him to always turn the elephant to face the door, for luck. This advice pleased him immensely and he planned to incorporate it into his door-closing window-shutting ritual when he reclaimed the room, although in a room with three doors facing in different directions he remained uncertain about which was 'the' door. Still, he believed that one day some secret signal would be given to indicate which door the elephant should face. For the moment, he turned it to face the corner.

For all his kindness though, the man had habits which were not pleasant. He smelled and it was not nice like the rusty nails or the grease of the desk. It was a damp mouldy smell like a dirty wet dog or a saddlecloth caught in the rain. At table his hands shook so much that the boy would watch in fascination as more often than not he missed his mouth and the carrots would sail across the aunt's highly polished rosewood and mahogany floor. At such times the boy did not laugh. He was fascinated by a certain precision which hovered over the old man's actions. He soon discovered that every movement by the man, even those which were obviously stupid, functioned along lines of scientific exactitude gone slightly askew. There was also an element of habitual action, almost of ritual in whatever the old man did, and it gave the boy a strong sense of identification.

Sometimes with invisible string the old man formed elaborate cat's cradles. He knew them by heart for the pattern never varied. These activities seemingly required from the man almost total concentration, his mouth slightly open. At other times he simply sat still with his hands interlaced in his lap while his thumbs chased endless circles round each other. It was something the boy admired and practised in secret until he sometimes found himself doing it effortlessly and thoughtlessly like the old man. The man also had lucid times, when he would sit on the front verandah talking late into the night with the uncle. And one night at least, the boy in bed the other side of the house thought he heard the sound of uncontrolled weeping coming from the garden room. But he was too scared to investigate and wondered afterwards if he had really heard it.

At first he thought that the old man was unaware of his presence. Then after a while he saw that the man noticed him in a sly kind of way – sometimes when his cat's cradles had reached elaborate perfection he would turn to the boy and give him a nod of triumph as if to say 'ha'. At other times the old man would pass a limp hand vaguely in his direction. The old man, however, never spoke directly to him.

The boy did not mind. To him the old man was such an object of fascination that he seemed not quite ordinarily human. Rather, the boy imagined that he was like a space traveller in baggy clothes cast adrift from his planet and flung wondrously upon the lonely country house.

So fascinated was he by the old man that he no longer visited Bro. Justice. At first when he thought of his neglect of Bro. Justice he was supremely self-conscious, for he knew that the old man had usurped Bro. Justice's place in his life and that Bro. Justice was in some unspoken way, angry.

When he had first come to the aunt and uncle's, Bro. Justice was the only person with whom he felt comfortable. In that big house with the perpetual smell of wax, the heavy mahogany furniture, the glass windows, he felt displaced, as if he had been plucked from one world which was small and snug and mistakenly placed into another which was like a suit many times too large and to which he could never have hopes of growing to a perfect fit. And in an unspoken way the aunt seemed to criticise him for his failure to grow quickly enough to flesh out the suit. The uncle was kindly in a vague manner; there were times when he even indulged the boy, for it was not his sister, after all, who had made the disastrous marriage.

Now the aunt's relationship with Bro. Justice was double-edged. The aunt both feared Bro. Justice and grudgingly respected him, as the bully does anyone who defies. For Bro. Justice was a Rastafarian and the only reason she tolerated him at all was that Bro. Justice's father had been with the uncle since his father's time, and Bro. Justice under his father's tutelage had in his turn developed into one of the best cattle men in the parish. He had also been the best man on the Pen before he, according to the aunt, began to turn 'queer' with his beard and his matted hair and his Bible.

One night a passing Rastaman had stopped off at the barracks where the penmen lived. They viewed him first with alarm and then as a creature wondrous and strange for in those days Rastamen were a novelty. People had heard of this strange and dreaded group of men in the cities but the only ones ever seen in that part of the world were ones who would simply be passing through. It turned out that this one, Bro. Naptali, had worked as a penman on the property at one time, though now he had grown almost unrecognisable to all who had known him. For three days and three nights Bro. Naptali stayed with them, leaving at the crack of dawn as mysteriously as he had come. While the rest of the men had treated him as a figure of derision, Bro. Justice had been deeply moved by his words and his demeanour. After Bro. Naptali left, Bro. Justice pondered on his words long and deeply. Then suddenly one day he took off for

5

no one knows where. He stayed away forty days and forty nights and suddenly, dramatically, reappeared as Bro. Justice.

Apart from his physical appearance, the thing that the aunt noticed and disliked most about Bro. Justice was the fact that in going away, he had lost that respect for others them which had been inculcated in men like him for centuries, and which the aunt at least considered only her due. While the other workers continued to address her as 'maam' and 'mistress', Bro. Justice refused to address her at all. He had withdrawn himself from the life of the Pen, confining his contact with others only to his duties, and retreated to the bottom of the citrus grove where he erected a little hut. After a while, so deeply did he burrow himself into his new life, that even the aunt stopped questioning his right to his own existence.

At first she did not know what to do about the boy's relationship with Bro. Justice. But since she herself had no idea what to do to entertain or amuse a boy child of that age, she did not interfere in case she might become saddled with the responsibility. She was thus pleased in a vindictive way when the old man came to stay and, for the time being anyway, so attracted the child's attention that he seemed to have completely forgotten about the Rastafarian.

Now, just as the aunt thought, Bro. Justice was angry about the boy's desertion for he had been extremely pleased about the way in which the child could sit for hours listening to his discourses, and in a sense considered the boy a potential disciple. The child was also a novelty in Bro. Justice's life, for as he got deeper and deeper into his religion, he found himself more and more distanced from the people around him, until he sometimes felt as remote from them as the furthest star. The boy alone had been able to enter his world, questioning only its superficial manifestations. The boy did not ask for or take anything from this world. The boy simply was.

He was also angry at the boy's defection because, simply, he missed him. For once the boy was gone he again had to contend with his own loneliness. But he was also upset for another reason: he did not like the old man. In fact he feared and

PRIDE

6

disliked the old man for a reason that shamed him deeply, something that had occurred while his father was still alive and he was a young boy about the Pen, and something which he never liked to think about. And ever after that he had always taken pains to keep out of the man's way whenever he came for his nerves.

He had been coming each year for his nerves as long as Bro. Justice could remember. In the early days though, nothing seemed too wrong with him, he was then a good-looking man, probably the uncle's age though now he looked twice as old. He would spend endless hours walking about the property aimlessly. The thing that Bro. Justice never liked to think about was this: it was the way the man used to watch him. Even in those days before he became religious, Bro. Justice felt instinctively that for one man to look at another man like that was sinful. As a youngster, Bro. Justice had the jobs around the yard – feeding the young calves, looking after the chickens, helping the aunt with her vegetable garden. He could not escape from the gaze of this man. Even when he was fully occupied with his chores he could feel the man watching him, would turn suddenly and there the man would be. He knew the man was not watching the chickens or what he was doing. He was watching *him*. And watching him the way he should be watching a woman. Bro. Justice went out of his way to avoid the man. Once the two of them coming in opposite directions approached the narrow gate which led to the backyard at the same time and as Bro. Justice shrunk into the narrow space to let him pass, the man had actually reached out and lightly touched his face. Bro. Justice instinctively drew away and the man did nothing else as he continued past but turn his head sideways and smile at him. The smile held a threat or a promise and Bro. Justice wanted to kill him. For years afterwards whenever the image of the man came to his mind the blood would fly to his head and he would want to annihilate that smile.

But that was really a long time ago. With the passing years, the man had seemed more frail, less assured, and even though he still walked over the property it was with the unsure steps of a spacewalker. And as he became more pathetic, Bro. Justice, remembering Job, softened towards him, although he still carefully maintained a distance. After a while he had even forgotten his earlier, even childish fear of the man for he had, after all, done him no harm. But now the man had come again, for his nerves, and the boy was also here, and this configuration disturbed Bro. Justice profoundly.

Bro. Justice was given to deep concentration counterbalanced by sudden and sometimes irrational action. Now, he reasoned deeply with himself on the subject. His reasoning did not help him. So distressed did he become that he took the unbelievable step of going to the aunt herself to plead with her please look after the little boy. But the aunt, immensely pleased that Bro. Justice had finally felt the need to approach her, took it as an occasion to lecture him about his appearance, his manners, his attitude, and in their double conversation which came to be conducted loudly and simultaneously, heard nothing of his mutterings of 'Sodom', 'sin', or the foolishness that is bound up in the heart of a child.

Indeed, when she afterwards remembered a few words of the conversation she dismissed them as part of Bro. Justice's jealousy at being supplanted in the eyes of the child, and she rejoiced at his discomfort. Bro. Justice could have called the child and seduced him back from the old man but he was too proud lest the boy think he could not continue life without him. So Bro. Justice ended up doing the only thing he could, and that was to attempt to keep the boy and the old man constantly under his eye. Whereas before he used to sit in his hut in the afternoons, he now took to sitting motionless underneath the house which rose on stilts at the back. His favourite perch was on a large smooth rock immediately beneath the garden room where he was hidden by the steps leading into the garden. He quietened his spirit by deciding that if ever the child should be in danger, Jehovah-Jah would give him a sign – any sign. In the meantime, his machete beside him, he pursued earnestly his reading of the Bible.

The boy and the old man had taken to spending a lot of time

in the room where the old man would rest and the boy, when he thought the man was asleep, would try and recapture some of the magic of the room by rifling the pigeonholes. But there were times when all the life with which he had once imbued the objects in the room seemed drained from them by the old man and his mysterious 'nerves'. The boy did not know what nerves were except that they were alive and he could feel them pulsating in the room like telegraph wires. The hum occurred even when the old man was sleeping which he thought strange – until he discovered that frequently the man wasn't sleeping at all but was surreptitiously watching him beneath half-closed eyes. At first this made him feel strange and uncomfortable and he wished himself safe back in Bro. Justice's hut. But he did not leave the room. For one thing he was now ashamed to go back to Bro. Justice. Besides, something told him that if he once deserted, then even when the man left, he would never again in any shape or form be able to reclaim the room again.

So he continued to watch the man and to visit the room while he was there. But now he knew that the man was watching him, he grew more conscious of himself, and of the man. Sometimes sitting at the desk he would quickly turn toward the bed and feel triumphant if he caught the old man quickly closing his eyes. At other times when he was sure the man was sleeping because he could hear his thin snores, he would go and stand by the bed and look down on the unshaven face and try to summon up a feeling of power to counteract the nerves flowing through him. But when the old man was awake he kept a physical distance from him for over time he felt that the old man was gradually drawing him in towards him, probably by means of his mysterious nerves. And he sensed that the old man would one day draw close enough to touch him even as he feared that if this ever happened, everything – Bro. Justice, the room, the magic world, even the order of the aunt and uncle's life that he both loved and despised – would be lost to him forever and he too might thereafter be condemned to float wonderingly in time and space in a suit many times too large.

Then one afternoon as usual the old man was having his rest

in the darkened room. The boy crept in and started to play with the objects in the uncle's desk, the semi-precious stones, the rusted nails, the official papers, and the box level. He played this game frequently: first he would try to get the eye in the box level perfectly in the centre and this was hard for the desk top sloped, and then he would try to project his mind deep into this eye so that he could reach through to the mysterious world he felt certain existed beyond. He was so engaged in this game that he did not hear the old man. Rather he first sensed his presence, then felt his breath. The boy jumped from the chair, setting the box level askew, for the old man standing so close to him was no longer looking coy or foolish. His hair was standing untidily from his head as always, his dirty merino collar rose above his shirt, and he smelled the same way, but his eyes were no longer weak and uncertain. They were firmly focussed on the boy and they held a command. All through his body the boy suddenly felt drained and weak. Through a film like that covering the eye of the spirit level he saw the man advance towards him.

He stepped backwards, his heart beating wildly, and on the window sill his hand encountered a tiny object – it was the ivory elephant. Instinctively, he turned it to face the door leading to the garden through which he felt any moment now would come Bro. Justice and his shiny machete, even though there was in the sky more than a hint of summer lightning. But his heart was pounding out a message so loudly that he knew no matter where Bro. Justice was, or the state of the weather, he was bound to receive it.

Love Orange

Work out your own salvation with fear and trembling.
Phillipians

SOMEWHERE between the repetition of Sunday School lessons and the broken doll which the lady sent me one Christmas I lost what it was to be happy. But I didn't know it then even though in dreams I would lie with my face broken like the doll's in the pink tissue of a shoebox coffin. For I was at the age where no one asked me for commitment and I had a phrase which I used like a talisman. When strangers came or lightning flashed, I would lie in the dust under my grandfather's vast bed and hug the dog, whispering "our worlds wait outside" and be happy.

Once I set out to find the worlds outside, the horizon was wide and the rim of the far mountains beckoned. I was happy when they found me in time for bed and a warm supper, for the skies, I discovered, were the same shade of China blue as the one intact eye of the doll. "Experience can wait," I whispered to the dog, "death too".

I knew all about death then because in dreams I had been there. I also knew a great deal about love. Love, I thought, was like an orange, a fixed and sharply defined amount, limited, finite. Each person had this amount of love to distribute as he may. If one had many people to love then the segments for each person would be smaller and eventually love, like patience, would be exhausted. That is why I preferred to live with my grandparents then since they had fewer people to love than my parents and so my portion of their love-orange would be larger.

My own love-orange I jealously guarded. Whenever I thought of love I could feel it in my hand, large and round and brightly coloured, intact and spotless. I had moments of indecision when I wanted to distribute the orange but each time I would grow

11

afraid of the audacity of such commitment. Sometimes, in a moment of rare passion, I would extend the orange to the dog or my grandmother but would quickly withdraw my hand each time. For without looking I would feel in its place the doll crawling into my hand and nestling there and I would run into the garden and be sick. I would see its face as it lay in the pink tissue of a shoebox tied with ribbons beside the stocking hanging on the bedpost and I would clutch my orange tighter, thinking that I had better save it for the day when occasions like this would arise again and I would need the entire orange to overcome the feelings which arose each time I thought of the doll.

I could not let my grandmother know about my being sick because she never understood about the doll. For years I had dreamed of exchanging homemade dolls with button eyes and ink faces for a plaster doll with blue eyes and limbs that moved. All that December I haunted my grandmother's clothes closet until beneath the dresses I discovered the box smelling faintly of camphor and without looking I knew that it came from Miss Evangeline's toy shop and that it would therefore be a marvel. But the doll beside the Christmas stocking, huge in a billowing dress and petticoats, had half a face and a finger missing. "It can be mended," my grandmother said, "I can make it as good as new. 'Why throw away a good thing?' Miss Evangeline said as she gave it to me."

But I could no longer hear I could no longer see for the one China blue eye and the missing finger that obscured my vision. And after that I never opened a box again and I never waited up for Christmas. And although I buried the box beneath the allamanda tree the doll rose up again and again, in my throat, like a sickness to be got rid of from the body, and I felt as if I too were half a person who could lay down in the shoebox and sleep forever. But on awakening from these moments, I would find safely clutched in my hands the orange, conjured up from some deep part of myself, and I would hug the dog saying "our worlds wait outside"

That summer I saw more clearly the worlds that awaited. It

was filled with many deaths that seemed to tie all the strands of my life together and which bore some oblique relationship to both the orange and the doll.

The first to die was a friend of my grandparents who lived nearby. I sometimes played with her grandchildren at her house when I was allowed to, but each time she had appeared only as a phantom, come on the scene silently, her feet shod in cotton stockings rolled down to her ankles, thrust into a pair of her son's broken down slippers. In all the years I had known her I had never heard her say anything but whisper softly; her whole presence was a whisper. She seemed to appear from the cracks of the house, the ceiling, anywhere, she made so little noise in her coming, this tiny, delicate, slightly absurd old woman who lived for us only in the secret and mysterious prison of the aged.

When she died it meant nothing to me, I could think then only of my death which I saw nightly in dreams but I could not conceive of her in the flesh, to miss her or to weep tears.

The funeral that afternoon was 5.00 p.m. on a hot summer's day. My grandmother dressed me all in white and I trailed down the road behind her, my corseted and whaleboned grandmother lumbering from side to side in a black romaine dress now shiny in the sunlight, bobbing over her head a huge black umbrella. My grandfather stepped high in shiny black shoes and a shiny black suit ahead of her. Bringing up the rear, I skipped lightly on the gravel, clutching in my hand a new, shiny, bright and bouncy red rubber ball. For me, the funeral, any occasion to get out of the house was a holiday, like breaking suddenly from a dark tunnel into the sunlight where gardens of butterflies waited.

They had dug a grave in the red clay by the side of the road. The house was filled with people. I followed my grandparents and the dead woman's children into the room where they had laid her out, unsmiling, her nostrils stuffed with cotton. I stood in the shadows where no one saw me, filled with the smell of something I had never felt before, like a smell rising from the earth itself which no sunlight, no butterflies, no sweetness could combat. "Miss Aggie, Miss Aggie," I said silently to the dead old woman and suddenly I knew that if I gave her my orange to take into the unknown with her it would be safe, a secret between me and one who could return no more. I gripped the red ball tightly in my hands and it became transformed into the rough texture of an orange; I tasted it on my tongue, smelled the fragrance. As my grandmother knelt to pray I crept forward and gently placed between Miss Aggie's closed hands the love-orange, smiled because we knew each other and nothing would be able to touch either of us. But as I crept away my grandmother lifted her head from her hands and gasped when she saw the ball. She swiftly retrieved it while the others still prayed and hid it in her voluminous skirt. But when she sent me home, in anger, on the way the love-orange appeared comforting in my hand, and I went into the empty house and crept under my grandfather's bed and dreamt of worlds outside.

The next time I saw with greater clarity the vastness of this world outside. I was asked to visit some new neighbours and read to their son. He was very old, I thought, and he sat in the sunshine all day, his head covered with a calico skull cap. He couldn't see very clearly and my grandmother said he had a brain tumour and would perhaps die. Nevertheless I read to him and worried about all the knowledge that would be lost if he did not live. For every morning he would take down from a shelf a huge Atlas and together we would travel the cities of the world to which he had been. I was very happy and the names of these cities secretly rolled off my tongue all day. I wanted very much to give him my orange but held back. I was not yet sure if he were a whole person, if he would not recover and need me less and so the whole orange would be wasted. So I did not tell him about it. And then he went off with his parents to England, for an operation, my grandmother said, and he came back only as ashes held on the plane by his mother. When I went to the church this time there was no coffin, only his mother holding this tiny box which was so like the shoe box of the doll that I was sure there was some connection which I could not grasp but I thought, if they bury this box then the broken doll cannot rise again.

But the doll rose up one more time because soon my grandmother lay dying. My mother had taken me away when she fell too ill and brought me back to my grandmother's house, even darker and more silent now, this one last time. I went into the room where she lay and she held out a weak hand to me, she couldn't speak so she followed me with her eyes and I couldn't bear it. "Grandma," I said quickly, searching for something to say, something that would save her, "Grandma, you can have my whole orange," and I placed it in the bed beside her hand. But she kept on dying and I knew then that the orange had no potency, that love could not create miracles. "Orange," my grandmother spoke for the last time trying to make connections that she did not see, "orange......?" and my mother took me out of the room as my grandmother died. "At least," my mother said, "at least you could have told her that you loved her, she waited for it".

"But..." I started to say and bit my tongue, for nobody, not then or ever could understand about the orange. And in leaving my grandmother's house, the dark tunnel of my childhood, I slammed the car door hard on my fingers and as my hand closed over the breaking bones, felt nothing.

Country Of The One Eye God

SHE heard the news on the little transistor radio her grand-daughter had sent her from the States. She who had lived so long she felt drained of all emotion, now experienced nothing but a confirmation of the news which had come floating down in scraps and whispers last year: her grandson was a thief, a murderer, a hired gunman, a rapist, a jailbird, a jail breaker, and now, at nineteen, a man with a price on his head.

From the time the first scraps of news had made their way from town, even as she expressed disbelief to keep up appear-ances, she knew that everything they said about him was the truth. She firmly believed that every evil deed, evil thought, of all the generations had finally been distilled into this one boy. Ever since the beginning when he had left home, she had coldly cast her mind back to every thing she knew about every single member of the family to discern if there was something hidden in her tribe that betokened this ending, and she could find nothing that warranted such a hard and final cruelty. They had faced deaths starvation hurricane earthquake cholera typhoid malaria tuberculosis fire diptheria and travel to dangerous and distant places in search of work. But beyond everything that they did, Ma Bell saw them as nothing more than victims struggling against the forces of a God who was sometimes deaf and blind.

Still, Ma Bell found the Lord a comforting presence. Since the last grandchild had left - the rapist, the thief, the hired gun, the murderer - Ma Bell had got into the habit of talking directly to the Lord. He was everywhere. She spent so much of her life in the consolation of his company that she could easily conduct dialogue with him for she knew his answers so well. And without having to let him know her whereabouts, she could continue her conversation with him anywhere in the house, in the yard, walking slowly and painfully down the lane to the Pentecostal Church of Christ the Redeemer. All her life, since she had first given birth at sixteen, sixty years ago, Ma Bell had spent her time addressing children and she saw nothing incongruous about addressing the Lord in the same manner for he failed her and tested her as surely as they did. Now she addressed him on the subject uppermost in her mind:

"Is wanting to better yuself a sin? Then if is sin, we have sinned. But nothing more than that. I know yu going pick on me first. But dont bother. If I did give short in my higglering days it was because I needed it, Lord. Pickney a yard needing shoes and books and clothes so they could learn to hold their head up high. And dont you see that it was right after all? Look how they turn out. Dont you please? Granted them forget me. You even. They dont write. Sometime I would starve if it was for them. Once in a blue moon a get a letter with a two, three dollar. But Lord, I ever get news yet that any of them in prison? That any of them thief? That any of them is murderer? Eh? You answer me that for you know even more than I hear. Never mind that I take their children and raise them till their mumma and puppa get establish in foreign and sometime when they done get establish they forget all we poor one still a scuffle down here. But dont you think a little cutting corner here and there is worth it? Talk truth now."

"Ma B, Ma B," a hurried and anxious voice called from the doorway "You hear the news?"

"Come in, Jacob. Dont excite up yuself so. Yu know is not good for the pressure."

"Ma B you did have yu radio on? Yu hear the news bout Jacko? Ma B, two thousand dollar reward."

Jacob was Ma Bell's seventy-year-old nephew but since he had never acquired her calm, she treated him just like a boy.

She now said patiently, "Yes Jacob. Jacko is now big wanted man. So what yu expect me to do?"

17

"But Ma B yu dont see what going to happen?"

"What, Jacob Sawyers?"

"If him on the run where the first place yu think him come?"

"Well if you think is here yu is a bigger fool than I think."

"How yu mean, dont is you grow him?"

"Jacob Sawyers, yu know that I never hear one living word from Jacko from December eighteen gone two year now him tief mi little coffee money and tek off. That is how him treat him gran that raise him from him born. But that blood in him was bad from the start. A beat and a beat and it never come out. A never see a child come tough so. Yu could beat Jacko from morning till night and not a drop of eye water ever come. Is the times breeding them tough pickney. But he dont get no bad blood from my family I dont have to tell you. And he would have nerves coming here. Nobody in this family was ever a criminal. Nobody ever a thief. And I can go back five generation to my mother Iris Jestina Howell born in 1884 the same year as Bustamante and to her mother Myrtelle Dawkin Nathan born in 1863 and fe her mother Lucilda who was born a slave and get her emancipate from Queen Victoria with the rest of the slave them 1838. And on your side of the family my lawful husband Nathaniel Jacob Sawyers and his father Isiah Sawyers and his father father Lemonius Sawyers that go to Colón in 1849. All their generation. Not one is robber. Not one is thief. Not one raise gun or other implement against other human being so earn money. No. Mark you I never encourage my son when he start courting that Carter gal for everbody round here know that them not a family that can hold up their head for reason I dont have to go into. But it not nice. But Jacob, never on this earth there is a generation like thisa one. They is truly a generation of vipers. But God see and know everything and one day one day, Jacob. But how they come so eh? How we that dont do nobody nothing bring children into world and before them old enough to spit, is animal them turn?"

"O Ma B evil evil evil in this land."

"A-men."

"But it predick you know Ma B. As the Good Book say Job Thirtieth Verse Twelve upon my right hand rise the youth they push away my feet and raise up against me the ways of their destruction."

"Ah Jacob, true word."

"But Ma B, if him come here. What yu going to do?"

"Jacob Sawyers, dont vex mi spirit ya. The boy have him combolo all over the place. No dem he did run way with. Mek him go to them."

But even as Ma Bell spoke she could feel the thread that bound her grandson to her rewinding, tightening around her heart. With every tremor of a sunset cloud which came together, melted and dissolved, with the chirping of a tree frog, the flicker of a pennie-wallie, she felt her heart leap, had a premonition of the world all cata-corner and moving off course.

The boy came near dawn when she had almost given up expecting him. She knew that now with a price on his head if he did not come tonight he probably would never come again. When she heard the scratching at her door, Ma Bell was pleased that after all the call of blood remained so strong, even as she feared to open her door to this stranger. For stranger he was. In the pale moon glow, for she was afraid to bring the lamp to the door lest it attract her neighbours, she saw a bearded and hairy stranger with a countenance that would frighten children. She could discern nothing of family in this person and for a moment feared that it was in fact a stranger come to do her harm. But from the familiar way he came into the house she knew that it was he.

"So yu came?"

"What yu expect?"

"Dont yu have friend?"

"Fren a dawg."

"Is friend yu run away with from here."

"Ol lady, that time so long ago it long like from here to moon."

Even his voice had changed and it was not only that it had deepened with age but it held an edge of bitterness even as it suggested the weariness of an old man.

She didn't know what to expect and wasn't sure about why she wanted the boy here. But she thought that even though he was now a man with a price on his head beyond any sum she had ever conceived of owning in her life, she was still his gran and had a right to expect a show of respect, even warmth, from him. But not this cold detachment.

He followed her into the kitchen attached to the house at the back and carefully put the latch on the door. From beneath the ashes of the fireplace she unearthed the roast yam and from a pan on the fireside took a piece of fried saltfish which she put on top of the yam as the 'rider'. Ma Bell had known that at whatever hour he came he would be hungry. He wolfed down the food like a starving man while from the battered thermos she poured him a mug of sweetened bissy.

"Nuh have no rum?"

"Rum? Listen no bwoy. Just because yu is bull buck and duppy conqueror everywhere else yu is still bwoy in this yard. So just know yu place. Rum in this house is big man sinting."

Without answering or looking at her he coolly stretched across to the tiny kitchen cupboard and took out a flask of white rum which he knew she always kept there as a medicine against cold, fevers and a wetting in the rain. He put the flask to his head and drank, then set it down on the table in front of him while he finished eating.

Ma Bell shrank away. Never before in her house had anyone shown such a lack of manners, for if the children she raised acquired nothing else, it was manners that she hammered into their heads from birth.

"A need some money."

O God O God she asked herself. Is family this? This is what it come to Lord? O rid me and deliver me from the hands of strange children whose mouth speaketh vanity and their right hand is the right hand of falsehood.

"What yu want money for? Nobody can help you now. Only Jesus can help you."

He sucked his teeth.

"A haffe leave."

"Leave? Go where?"

"Where yu think? Yu think is holiday I come spend?"

"How far yu think yu can get?"

"You dont worry. I have mi passport."

"What? Yu plan to go to foreign?"

"What else? Dont I have mother, dont I have father in foreign?"

"Jesus no. You wouldnt go over there and bring no shame on them Jacko. No. They been fighting all their life over there to lift their head up. Even if I had it I would never give you money to see yu shame them and them family."

"Oh. So me not family? Them never shame me? Them never shame me when they walk way leave me? Look how long I wait for them to send for me and all I ever hear is next year next year. Next year never did came for me for every year them breed up a new pickney. They could never afford to send for me. Well, long time now I decide to start take my next year this year. I couldnt wait no more."

"Jacko. No. How yu so bold. Keep yu badness to yuself. Turn yourself in and take your punishment. Dont inflict it on anybody else."

"Is bury you want bury me alive. Me hear enough talk and get enough battering from you when I small. Mi no need no more talk any more. Just give me the money - thats all I come for."

"Where yu expect an old woman like me to get money?"

"A who yu a talk to? Dont your whole generation dem in foreign. Yu was always proud of that. Not like we poor one that turn down back here."

She was suddenly afraid, hardly listening to what he was saying, wondering if Jacko when he lived with her had somehow discovered the secret that nobody knew – where she kept her money. For Ma Bell did have a cache of money which she hoarded for a purpose. Every extra cent she could squeeze from her frugal living she kept in this special fund. She kept this money for one reason only. When Ma Bell died, she wanted the most beautiful coffin that the undertaker could provide - the real undertaker from town and not Brother Bertie who sent off everyone around in plain cedar coffins. The coffin was some-thing that Ma Bell had to provide for herself; she did not believe that anyone in her family would go to that sort of expense when she was not around to see. Ma Bell had arrived at the decision about the coffin late in life when she saw that none of her other secret longings would ever be fulfilled. Ma Bell used to say to the Lord:

"Poor people just come into world so and is just so they must leave? Well I ent leaving that way and I dont care if you dont like it."

She wanted to leave this world and enter the next cocooned in the luxury she never had in life and she sometimes grew impatient at the slowness with which the fund had accumulated for she was anxious to lie in the splendour of white satin surrounded by polished wood and silver fittings, in a coffin so heavy it would take twelve men to lift it. Ma B hoped that the undertaker would make her face beautiful at last so that every-one for miles around would come to ooh and aah as they walked past the open coffin where she lay in state. That is why she became fearful at the boy's mention of money for she would rather die than part with it.

Ma Bell kept this money in a long piece of cloth which she rolled and tied round her waist. Also in the cloth in her spidery handwriting on thin paper were her most careful instructions for her burial. Like all old women, Ma Bell had such a collection of baggy old clothes and bits of string and cloth tied around her that no one ever suspected that her garments held a secret.

The boy had finished the food and was leaning back in her one good chair. Ma Bell searched his face to see in it the signs that would tell her that this was one of the most wanted criminals in the country but could discern nothing that set him apart from the boys his age around except for an assurance of manner and a hardness in his eyes. He had a presence that forced even his grandmother to look away. She shivered, and knew that someone had walked over her grave. In the pale light, Ma Bell suddenly wondered how such a little boy could suddenly grow so huge as to fill all the spaces in the room. She felt shrivelled and light, compressed into the interstices of space by his nearness.

"Money", he said again.

Ma Bell said nothing but abruptly rose and squeezed past him into the room where she slept and came back with a cocoa tin stuffed full of papers which she emptied on the table. Coins rolled on to the floor and the papers turned out to be old envelopes and scraps wrapped around the small sums she apportioned for her various needs.

"Seetya, You can have all of it. Three dollar that I was saving to pay doctor on the bill I owe him. Two dollar buy a little soup bone from Ba Daniel Saturday. One dollar eighteen cent for my tithe O God you wouldnt take that is the Lord's money. This is five dollar I just get from the fowl I sell Jestina Dawson."

She was muttering to herself as she slowly unrolled each bit of money but the boy said nothing, looking only with anxious eyes to see if there was more. His grandmother, sensing this anxiety for a moment felt a surge of power over him. He searched beneath the table for the coins which had fallen and including the tithe money over her protests, counted all there was.

"Twenty-eight dollar two cents. Cho. How far yu expect me to get with that? I cant reach anybody else with money now Babylon a watch them. Just bring out the real dunza ya."

"Jacko. Dont try mi patience. Blood or no blood bother me long enough and a bawl out fe murder so loud that every single soul for ten mile bout hear me."

"Yeah. A would like to see you bawl for once for all the bawling you mek me do in my life. That is all your generation ever know to do. How to drop lick and chastisement."

"Jacko, you have walked far from the ways of the Lord. My heart bleed to see what you turn into. But it is not too late to

23

repent and give yourself up. Judgement Day must begin at the house of the Lord."

The boy laughed a sneering laugh.

"Nutten change, eh? Same ol foolishness bout God and judgement. That is the trouble with the whole lot a unno. All unno think bout is judgement and future life. But from morning me study seh in this country fe yu God is a one eye God. Him only open him good eye to people who have everything already so him can pile up more thing on top of that. Him no business with rag tag and bobtail like unno. God up a top a laugh keh keh keh at the likes of you. Fe see you, so poor and turn down think you can talk to the likes of him so high and mighty. Keh keh keh."

"Jacko!"

"Fe yu God ever help anybody yu know?"

"Plenty time."

"Yes? Well yu better start pray to him from now that yu remember where yu put the money. Or yu want me to search for it?"

"Jacko. No. Dont do this to your old gran."

Ignoring her, he started slowly, methodically, to search the house. There was not much to search, for apart from the kitchen Ma Bell had only two rooms. The boy searched every pot, every vase, every shelf, turned out drawers, battered trunks, cardboard boxes and pressed-paper suitcases sitting in the rafters. He pulled the bed and the mattress apart, lifted all the loose floorboards that he remembered as a child, and turned out the cheese tins in which were growing on the little verandah a few half-dead plants. He took the photographs out of their frames, held Ma Bell's Bible and shook it, and to her everlasting shame, rummaged among her stiffly starched and pressed undergarments. He conducted the search swiftly and silently, carrying the small kerosene lamp from room to room. Ma Bell followed like a sleepwalker. It never occurred to her to run, to cry out to her neighbours, or to plead with the boy. She suddenly felt very old and with the pounding which had started up in her ears, began to see and hear things as from a great distance. She felt the thread around her heart tightening and tightening so she could hardly breathe. Ma Bell followed her grandson through his path of destruction as if he had already robbed her of her speech, her mind, her bodily strength, her will.

When the boy had finished his search they found themselves back in the kitchen where they started as if there was a certain logic in this night that drew them tightly in this circle.

"OK Ma B. A giving you one more chance. I aint quick to fire blow like yu. A dont even want to hurt yu. But is hard time we living in now and if yu wont give the money to me, a dont care no more. A will find it and take it."

"I have no money my son," Ma Bell said in a weak voice.

"Rass. Dont give me that. Me know unno old woman. Yu have the money hide on yu."

"I have no money, Jacko. Dont shame me so."

"Ma B, for the last time, give me the money. Yu soon dead and lef it yu know. What you want money for? Let it go nuh. I have the whole of my life still in front of me. Nah give up so."

Ma B said nothing but closed her eyes.

"Please God O please God dont let what him saying about you be true. That you is a one eye God. I know better than that. Show him what you can do. No matter what he say, dont let him get my burial money. That is my future. O God deliver me from this snare that bind me."

When she opened her eyes she saw without astonishment that the boy was pointing a gun at her.

"No. If you shoot me Jacko, yu will never leave this place alive. Everybody will hear that gun."

"Let me worry about that. Me sure no God going to hear yu. This is the country of the one-eye God. And he a-see neither you nor me. Ma B, a giving you one more chance. Give me the money. For a not fighting with you. A know you have it, and if a dont get it from you live a wi tek it from you dead."

"Please God, a know you think is vanity. But I truly dont want to go into the next world as poor and naked as I come into this one. Please God, no matter what happen, dont let him find my burial money. God, he is my very blood. He wouldnt really kill me? Eh God?"

Ma Bell prayed and prayed as the boy carefully lifted the gun.

Ascot

"THAT Ascot goin go far," Mama say, "Mark my word".

"Yes. Him goin so far him goin ennup clear a prison," Papa say. Every time you mention Ascot name to Papa these days the big vein in Papa forehead tighten up and you know he trying hard to control himself.

"Oh gawd when all is said an done the bwoy do well Jackie. Doan go on so," Mama say.

"De bwoy is a livin criminal. Do well me foot. Look how him treat him family like they have leprosy. Deny dem. Is so you wan you pickney behave. Cho woman. Yu was always a fool," and with that Papa jam him hat on him head and take off down the road.

See here! I dont think Papa ever recover from the day that Ascot come back. This Ascot is a tall red bwoy that born round here. Mama and all the rest of the women did like Ascot who is Miss Clemmy outside son for Ascot come out with fair skin and straight nose and though him hair not so good it not so bad neither. And nobody know who Ascot father is but is not Dagoman who Miss Clemmy living with all these years for you only have to look at Dagoman to see that.

Anyhow this Ascot tall no langilalla and him not so bad looking though him have a mouth so big that when him smile him lip curl but all the women melt when Ascot smile and say how him bound to go far.

But all that the men remember bout Ascot is that Ascot is a real ginnal and also that Ascot have the biggest foot that anybody round here ever see. Especially Papa.

One time Papa use to miss all kind of thing from the buttery.

Now when Papa not looking all we children would tief in there and take two finger ripe banana or some small thing but nothing serious. Papa would find out and accuse we and we would lie but none of we could lie so good because Mama use to beat the lying out of we and Papa would know the culprit right away so nobody would take it serious. Papa use to say he wouldn't grudge his own children nothing, but is the principle of the thing and he dont like to have his authority undermine and that sort of thing.

Well, anyway, one time a whole heap of big thing start disappear from the buttery – a brand new cutlass, some yam head, a crocus bag and finally, a big bunch of banana that Papa was ripening for the church Harvest Festival. Well sah, all we children used to run in the buttery and look at the bunch of banana till we eye water but none of us would bold enough to touch it for is the most beautiful thing that we ever see in our whole life.

So the Saturday morning before the Harvest Festival one bangarang no bus at the house! Papa go into the buttery and the whole bunch of banana no gone way clean. Jesus. You should hear the noise he make. Then him calm down and he just stand there a look at the ground for a long time and is sad we think Papa sad for is the best bunch of banana that he ever grow. But finally him say, "All right. Is Ascot do it. See him guilt there plain as day. Is Ascot one have foot that size". And is true for we all look at the footprint on the ground and we know is Ascot do it.

Papa say to we, "Doan say a word," and him send off to call Ascot while him close the buttery door and tell all of we go sit on the verandah like nothing happen. So Ascot come grinning as usual like him expecting food and Papa say, "Come Ascot me bwoy Harvest Festival pospone and we gwine nyam banana caan done tidday".

As Papa say the word "banana" Ascot not grinning so wide again and he say as if him deaf "Wha Mass Jackie?" and we all start giggle for him voice come out squeaky like muss-muss and Papa say, "Yes bwoy feas tidday". Then we all walk round to the buttery and Papa throw the door wide open and the first thing that everybody see is the hook where the banana was hanging up empty as night.

"Oh gawd where me Harvest Festival banana gaan-o," Papa shout out. "Ascot look ya me banana no gaan".

"Wha Mass Jackie," Ascot say but you could see that him hanging back. "Nutten could go so afta nobody bolnuf come in ya and walk weh wid yu banana".

Papa just stand there for a while as if him studying the situation and then him say, "Ascot me bwoy, yu and me gwine have to play poleece an search fe clues".

Meanwhile Papa there looking at the ground and then he make as if him just see the footprint and he say, "Ascot look here me bwoy," and by now Ascot look like shame-me-lady macca that just done step on. Papa say, "But wait Ascot. Puddon yu foot ya".

And Ascot bawl out "Laaad Mass Jackie is nuh me do it sah".

Papa say, "No? Den puddon yu foot ya yu tiefing brute," and make to grab after Ascot. But Ascot jump back so braps and fly off like streak lightning. And from that day on, Papa swear that him wash him hand of Ascot.

Ascot stay far from the house for a good while and anytime he see Papa him take off to bush for Papa walking bout and threatening to shoot him for him banana though you know after a time that Papa enjoying himself so much telling everybody how him frighten Ascot that you can see that him dont mind bout the banana so much after all. But Ascot really have no shame at all and little by little him start hang round the kitchen again when Papa not there and Mama would feed him till finally him round the house almost as often as before.

Anyway my big brother Kenny did come up from May Pen one Sunday and Ascot come up to him when Papa back turn and ask if he couldnt give him job as gardener. And as Kenny dont know bout the banana – and he must be the only person Papa forget to tell – Kenny say alright. And although Papa warn Kenny that him talking up trouble Mama say that at

28

heart Ascot is really a decent honest boy and that all he need is opportunity so when Kenny ready to leave Ascot arrive with him bundle and seat himself off in Kenny car please no puss!

"No matter how hard yu wuk an how much money yu make yu will nevva find shoes for dem doan mek dem in fe yu size," was Papa's last word to Ascot.

Well sah, as Papa predict Ascot dont stay long with Kenny. Little after Ascot gone there we get letter from Kenny say he sending Ascot home for Ascot dont want do nothing round the yard and all he do all day is jump behind the wheel of motor car the minute people back turn and make noise like say he driving. The letter arrive one day and the next day we get another letter say Ascot take his belonging and a few other things that didnt belong to him so maybe he on the way home and good riddance. Anyway, Ascot never turn up at all and Miss Clemmie getting ready to go out of her mind that he in trouble till she get message say Ascot in Kingston learning to drive.

Then one day, bout a year after, who arrive but Ascot. He wearing a shirt and tie and pants that too short but is alright because it allow you to see Ascot shoes better. Ascot no get shoes! See here, he wearing the biggest pair of puss boot that ever make. It big so till everybody from miles around run to look at Ascot foot in shoes like is the eight wonder of the world. Ascot tell we he driving car in Kingston though most people dont believe him. But mark you, from Ascot small he used to tell me how him life ambition was to dress up in white clothes and drive a big white car.

So Ascot stay round for a while doing not a thing and he not smiley-smiley so much and in fact Ascot get very quiet. Then one day him no announce that him get paper to go States as farm worker and the next day him leave us again dress up in him big brown puss boots.

Well it look like Ascot dead fe true this time for nobody hear from him till government send a man down to Miss Clemmie to find out if she hear from him for he skip the farm work in Florida and just disappear right after he reach. Poor Miss Clemmie frighten so till and crying the whole time now for

29

Ascot for the man say that they going to prison Ascot if they find him for he does do a criminal thing. But still not a word from Ascot and everybody give him up for dead or prison except Papa who say that the cat. which is the incarnation of the devil have nine life and that is Ascot. About three year pass and Miss Clemmie no get letter from the United States. She beg me read it to her and it say:

Dear Ma wel i am her in New York is Big plase and they have plenty car I am going to get one yr loving son Ascot.

And he enclose one dollar and no return address. About two year pass and then Miss Clemmie get another letter from the USA which she beg me read. Is from Ascot and it say:

Dear mother wel here I am in Connecticut. Connecticut is Big plais. I driveing car two year now but is not wite yr loving son Ascot.

And he sent two dollar. Then about a year later she get another letter that say:

Dear Mother Chicago is Big plais I drevein wite car for a wite man but he don make me where wite is black unform so I mite leave yr loving son Ascot.

And he send three dollar. "He-he," say Papa to Miss Clemmie, "by the time yu get fifty letter yu nuh rich". But Miss Clemmie dont laugh for she say she sure Ascot leading bad life. And that was the last time she get letter from Ascot.

After that so much time pass that all of we almost forget Ascot. One time Papa did get a little banana bonus so I go to town and come back with some nice meat and Papa go dig him good yam and the day after that we cook a backra dinner. Papa just sitting on the verandah making the smell kill him and telling me and Mama to hurry up. Next thing we know a big white car no draw up at the gate and turn into the yard. "Eheh is who dat?" Papa say and we all run to the verandah. All we can see is the front door open and two foot stick outside.

"Jesus have mercy is Ascot," Mama say, "is Ascot one have foot big so".

"Ascot me teet. Whe Ascot fe get big car from?" Papa say.

But lo and behold. No Ascot! Ascot dress in white from head

to toe and though him plenty fatter him teeth kin same way. And a woman get out of the car with him and you can see she foreign from the clothes she wearing and the colour of her hair though I swear afterward is wig.

Eh-eh, Ascot him no rush up to my mother and start hug and kiss her, "Aunt Essie, Aunt Essie," he crying.

"Aunt Essie," Papa say, "since when she anything but Miss Essie," but Ascot rushing to him a cry "Uncle Jackie" and next thing we know he hugging Papa who turn purple he so vex. "Cousin Lily" – thats me he talking to – and he there hugging me too before I know what is happening. Papa stand there with him mouth open like him seeing rolling calf but Ascot so busy a chat he dont notice.

"An this," he say, "is my wife Anthea" and the lady say hello in this deep American accent.

"Ascot then is really you," Mama saying and she look like she almost crying.

"Yes Aunt Essie is real wonderful to see you," Ascot say and his American accent so thick you could cut it with knife.

"Cousin Lily" he say, taking my hand, "Can I speak to you for a minute?" and he haul me off into the parlour. "Cousin Lily, you are my friend for a long time now. Right?" So I say "right". "Okay, so just pretend that you is my cousin and this is my house, right." Eheh I dont know what Ascot playing but this whole thing sweet me so I say OK and call Mama and tell her. Of course she dont understand what really going on so I keep my finger cross.

By the time I get back to the verandah Ascot is there like a man that make out of nothing but energy, is not the Ascot that leave here at all. He just walking and talking and moving his hand up and down the whole time. Then he say to the wife, "Come let me show you around my birthhouse," and next thing he leading her through the whole house as if is him own it. Mama just stand there with her jaw drop and Papa mouth set while the vein in him forehead beating hard. Then Ascot take the wife into the yard and he there waving him hand and telling her, "And this is my property and this is my coconut tree – you

31

ever see coconut tree with coconut before – and this is where I does bathe when I small and this is our water tank that I did help build".

See ya pappyshow! Well that was bad enough but next thing he gone to Papa cocoa tree and he there saying "And this is a cocoa tree from which you does get chocolate bet you never see that before," and he grab up Papa cutlass and chop off one of the cocoa pod and start cut it up to show her the seed.

Papa start to get up but Mama say "Jackie" and he just sink back down into the chair as if he defeated. Then Ascot and him wife came back on the verandah and sit down and Ascot cock up him foot on the railing. He start chatting away but Papa not opening him mouth and so Mama and me there carrying on conversation. Ascot say him driving him own big white car and he work in a garage but he like one of boss man now and he so happy that he had to bring his wife back to show her the birthplace where he spend his happy childhood. He also say they staying in hotel in Kingston and they going back that night and is rent they rent the car they driving. That was one thing but next thing I go ask the wife what she do and she announce that she is really a teacher but right now she just finishing up her Master Degree. Master Degree? – Ascot marry woman with Master Degree and he dont even finish third standard in school. See here Lord. We all speechless again.

So Ascot there chatting and chatting and we all getting hungrier and hungrier and the food smelling better and better and it dont look as if they out to leave so finally Mama say in her best speaky-spokey voice, "Would you like a bite to eat?" and I know is show off she showing off on Ascot wife who have Master Degree that she have good food in the house.

"Yes thank you Aunt Essie is long time since I taste you cooking," Ascot say and cross him leg. Papa give Mama such a look that thank God none of them did see. Mama never see neither she so please that she entertaining somebody with Master Degree for the highest qualified person she ever meet is Extension Officer and that dont count because is only agriculture him did learn. So we put out all the food that we did cook and Mama take out her best crockery and send down to Miss Melda to borrow the glasses that she did just get from her daughter-in-law in the States and everybody sit down to eat – everybody except Papa who say he not hungry and he dont want anything to eat and we know better than to argue with him when he vex like that.

Well sah. Ascot put down a piece of eating there that I couldn't describe to you and when he done the table clean as a whistle. As soon as they eat done Mama say, "Well Ascot I suppose you want to spend some time with Clemmie," and Ascot say "Clemmie – Oh yes" as if he just remember her and he jump up and say "soon be back" and drive off to see Miss Clemmie. I tell you that was the biggest piece of extraness I ever see because Miss Clemmie live in the next bend in the road and if we want to call her all we do is lean out the kitchen window and shout. But Ascot drive gone and he stay away a long time and I believe is to confuse him wife that Miss Clemmie live a long way away.

About half an hour afterward Ascot arrive with the car full with Miss Clemmie and Dagoman and all the children dress in their best clothes. Ascot say to him wife, "And this is Clemmie and Dagoman," and Dagoman lift his hat and bow and I swear Miss Clemmie drop a curtsey.

"Oh and do you live nearby," say the wife to Miss Clemmie.

"Yes maam, jus roun de corner."

"And are all these your children?"

"Yes'm Hascot is de heldes but is not de same fader."

The wife give Ascot a look to kill and is plain she never realise that is Ascot mother.

"But I did almost grow with Aunt Essie" Ascot say quick but you could see him turning red.

"Clemmie," my mother call her inside, "Look here Clemmie," she tell her, "is your daughter-in-law that what you calling her maam for. Dont keep on saying yes maam no maam to everything she say. You hear me."

"Yes maam," say Miss Clemmie and while I inside clearing the table all I can hear is Miss Clemmie saying "yes maam, no maam" to everything her daughter-in-law saying.

Miss Clemmie keep on looking at Ascot as if he is stranger and Dagoman sit on the bench outside as if he too fraid to come near the lady. The children start play round the car and make as if to open the door and Ascot snap at them so till my mother had to say "Hi Ascot is your own little brothers yu treating so."

"Half brother," Ascot say.

From then on things just get from bad to worse. Ascot look like he vex cant done at Clemmie and the wife and stepfather look like they vex cant done with Ascot. So finally Ascot say, "Come let me take you all home for I have to get back to Kingston tonight." But by this time Dagoman face set and he say he prefer to walk and Miss Clemmie and the children get into the car alone and even thought Miss Clemmie look like she going to cry you can still see that she feeling proud to have her son driving her in car. But as they drive off all we can hear is Ascot a shout at the children to take their dirty feet off the car seat.

By the time Ascot get back he grinning all over again but you can see that everybody feeling kind of shame and just waiting for him to go. So he finally jump up and start kiss we goodbye only when he put out his hand to Papa Papa wouldnt take it though he shake hands with the wife and talk nice to her for he say afterward that she was a nice mannersable woman and is a shame that she mix up with a criminal like Ascot. So at long last Ascot and his wife drive off the way they did come with plenty horn blowing and hand waving.

Mama was the only one that wave back though and long after the car out of sight she there waving and smiling. "That Ascot," she say, "fancy that. A wife with Master Degree. I did know he was goin get far you know".

"Well he can stay far de next time," Papa shout and walk out of the house.

Next day it all over the district how Miss Clemmie have daughter-in-law with Master Degree and how Ascot prosper and hire big car and staying at hotel in Kingston. But is only me one Miss Clemmie did tell how there was not a bite to eat in the house that day and Ascot never even leave her a farthing. This vex me cant done especially how he did gormandise up all Papa food. So right then and there I start tell her what kind of good-fe-nutten Ascot is. And is only afterward that I realise that Miss Clemmie not listening to a word I saying.

"Dat Hascot. I did always know he wudda reach far yu know," she say almost to herself and her eyes shining like ackee seed.

Bright Thursdays

THURSDAY was the worst day. While she had no expectations of any other day of the week, every Thursday turned out to be either very good or very bad, and she had no way of knowing in advance which one it would be. Sometimes there would be so many bad Thursdays in a row that she wanted to write home to her mother, 'Please please take me home for I cannot stand the clouds'. But then she would remember her mother saying, "Laura this is a new life for you. This is opportunity. Now dont let yu mama down. Chile, swallow yu tongue before yu talk lest yu say the wrong thing and dont mek yu eye big for everything yu see. Dont give Miss Christie no cause for complain and most of all, let them know you have broughtuptcy."

Miss Christie was the lady she now lived with, her father's mother. She didn't know her father except for a photograph of him on Miss Christie's bureau where he was almost lost in a forest of photographs of all her children and grandchildren all brown skinned with straight hair and confident smiles on their faces. When she saw these photographs she understood why Miss Christie couldn't put hers there. Every week as she dusted the bureau, Laura looked at herself in the mirror and tried to smile with the confidence of those in the photographs, but all she saw was a being so strange, so far removed from those in the pictures, that she knew that she could never be like them. To smile so at a camera one had to be born to certain things – a big house with heavy mahogany furniture and many rooms, fixed mealtimes, a mother and father who were married to each other and lived together in the same house, who would chastise and praise, who would send you to school with the proper clothes so you would look like, be like everyone else, fit neatly into the space Life had created for you.

But even though others kept pushing her, and she tried to ease, to work her way into that space too, she sometimes felt that Life had played her tricks, and there was, after all, no space allotted for her. For how else could she explain this discomfort, this pain it caused her in this her father's house to confront even the slightest event. Such as sitting at table and eating a meal.

In her mother's house she simply came in from school or wherever and sat on a stool in a corner of the lean-to kitchen or on the steps while Mama dished up a plate of food which one ate with whatever implement happened to be handy. Mama herself would more often than not stand to eat, sometimes out of the pot, and the boys too would sit wherever their fancy took them. Everything would be black from the soot from the fireside which hung now like grotesque torn ribbons from the roof. After the meal, Laura would wash the plates and pots in an enamel basin outside and sweep out the ashes from the fireside. A meal was something as natural as breathing.

But here in this house of her father's parents a meal was a ritual, something for which you prepared yourself by washing your hands and combing your hair and straightening your dress before approaching the Table. The Table was in the Dining Room and at least twelve could have comfortably sat around it. Now Laura and the grandparents huddled together at one end and in the sombre shadows of the room, Laura sometimes imagined that they so unbalanced the table that it would come toppling over on to them. At other times, when she polished the mahogany she placed each of the children of the household at a place around this table, along with their mother and father and their bewhiskered and beribboned grandparents who looked down from oval picture frames. When they were all seated, they fitted in so neatly in their slots that there was now no place left for her. Sometimes she didn't mind.

But now at the real mealtimes, the ghosts were no longer there and she sat with the old people in this empty echoing space. Each time she sat down with dread in her heart, for meal time was not a time to eat so much as a time for lessons in Table Manners.

First Mirie the cook would tinkle a little silver bell that would summon them to the dining room, and the house would stir with soft footsteps scurrying like mice and the swish of water in the basin. All the inhabitants of the house were washing and combing and straightening themselves in preparation for the Meal. She tried not to be the last one to the table for that was an occasion for chastisement. Then she had to remember to take the stiffly starched white napkin from its silver ring and place it in her lap.

"Now sit up straight, child. Don't slump so," Miss Christie would say as she lifted the covers off tureens. Miss Christie sat at the table uncovering dishes of food, but by the time Laura was served, her throat was already full and she got so confused that she would forget the knife and start to eat with her fork.

"Now dear, please use your knife. And don't cut your meat into little pieces all at once."

At the sulky look which came over Laura's face, Miss Christie would say, "You'll thank me for this one day you know, Laura. If you are going to get anywhere, you must learn how to do things properly. I just can't imagine what your mother has been doing with you all this time. How a child your age can be so ignorant of the most elementary things is beyond me."

The first time Miss Christie had mentioned her mother in this way, Laura had burst into tears and fled from the room. But now, remembering her mother's words, she refused to cry.

Laura's father had never married her mother. The question never came up for, said Myrtle without even a hint of malice in her voice, "Mr Bertram was a young man of high estate. Very high estate". She was fond of telling this to everyone who came to her house and did not know the story of Laura's father. How Mr Bertram had come visiting the Wheelers where Myrtle was a young servant. They had had what she liked to call 'a romance' but which was hardly even imprinted on Mr Bertram's mind, and Laura was the result. The fact that Mr Bertram was a man of 'high estate' had in itself elevated Miss Myrtle so far in her own eyes that no one else could understand how she could have managed to bear her sons afterwards for two undoubtedly humble fathers.

Laura had come out with dark skin but almost straight hair which Miss Myrtle did her best to improve by rubbing it with coconut oil and brushing it every day, at the same time rubbing cocoa butter into her skin to keep it soft and make it 'clear'. Miss Myrtle made the child wear a broad straw hat to keep off the sun, assuring her that her skin was 'too delicate'.

Miss Myrtle had no regrets about her encounter with Mr Bertram even though his only acknowledgement of the birth was a ten dollar note sent to her at the time. But then he had been shipped off to the United States by his angry parents and nothing further had been heard from him.

Miss Myrtle was unfortunate in her choice of fathers for her children for none of them gave her any support. She single-handedly raised them in a little house on family land and took in sewing to augment what she got from her cultivation of food for the pot and ginger for the market. She did not worry about the fate of her sons for they were after all, boys, and well able to fend for themselves when the time came. But her daughter was a constant source of concern to her, for a child with such long curly hair, with such a straight nose, with such soft skin (too bad it was so dark) was surely destined for a life of ease and comfort. For years, Miss Myrtle sustained herself with the fantasy that one day Laura's father would miraculously appear and take her off to live up to the station in life to which she was born. In the meantime she groomed her daughter for the role she felt she would play in life, squeezing things here and there in order to have enough to make her pretty clothes so that she was the best-dressed little girl for miles around. For the time being, it was the only gift of her heritage that she could make her.

Then after so many years passed that it was apparent even to Myrtle that Mr Bertram had no intention of helping the child, she screwed up her courage, aided and abetted by the entire

39

village it seemed, and wrote to Mr Bertram's parents. She knew them well, for Mr Bertram's mother was Mrs Wheeler's sister and in fact came from a family that had roots in the area.

Dear Miss Kristie

Greetings to you in Jesus Holy Name I trust that this letter will find that you an Mister Dolfy ar enjoin the best of helth. Wel Miss Kristie I write you this letter in fear and trimblin for I am the Little One and you are the Big One but I hope you will not take me too forrard but mr. Bertram little girl now nine year old and bright as a button wel my dear Mam wish you could see her a good little girl and lern her lesson wel she would go far in Life if she could have some Help but I am a Poor Woman! With Nothing! To Help I am in the fidls morning til night. I can tel you that in looks she take after her Father but I am not Asking Mr Bertram for anything I know. He have his Life to live for but if you can fine it in YourPower to do Anything for the little girl God Richest Blessing wil come down on You May the Good Lord Bles and Keep you Miss Kristie also Mas Dolfy. And give you a long Life until you find Eternal Rest Safe in the arms of the Savor Your Humble Servant
Myrtle Johnstone.

The letter caused consternation when it was received by the old people for they had almost forgotten about what the family referred to as 'Bertram's Mistake' and they thought that the woman had forgotten about it too. Although Myrtle was only 17 at the time and their son was 28, they had never forgiven what Miss Christie called the uppity black gal for seducing their son. "Dying to raise their colour all of them," Miss Christie had cried, "dying to raise their colour. That's why you can't be too careful with them". Now like a ghost suddenly materialising they could see this old scandal coming back to haunt them.

At first the two old people were angry, then as they talked about the subject for days on end, they soon dismissed their first decision which was to ignore the letter, for the little girl, no matter how common and scheming her mother was, was nevertheless family and something would have to be done about her. Eventually they decided on limited help—enough to salve their consciences but not too much so that Myrtle would get the idea that they were a limitless source of wealth. Miss Christie composed the first of her brief and cool letters to the child's mother.

> Dear Myrtle,
> In response to your call for help we are sending a little money for the child, also a parcel which should soon arrive. But please don't think that we can do this all the time as we ourselves are finding it hard to make ends meet. Besides, people who have children should worry about how they are going to support them before they have them.
> Yours Truly,
> Mrs. C. Watson

They made, of course, no reference to the child's father who was now married and living in New Jersey.

Myrtle was overjoyed to get the letter and the parcel for they were the tangible indications that the child's family would indeed rescue her from a life of poverty in the mountains. Now she devoted even more care and attention to the little girl, taking pains to remind her of the fineness of her hair, the straightness of her nose, and the high estate of her father. While she allowed the child to continue to help with the chores around the house, she was no longer sent on errands. When all the other children were busy minding goats, fetching water or firewood, all of these chores in her household now fell on Laura's brothers. Myrtle was busy grooming Laura for a golden future.

Because of her mother's strictures, the child soon felt alienated from others. If she played with other children, her mother warned her not to get her clothes too dirty. Not to get too burnt in the sun. Not to talk so broad. Instead of making her filled with pride as her mother intended, these attentions made the child supremely conscious of being different from the children around her, and she soon became withdrawn and lacking in spontaneity.

Myrtle approved of the child's new quietness as a sign of

'quality' in her. She sent a flood of letters to Miss Christie, although the answers she got were meagre and few. She kept her constantly informed of the child's progress in school, of her ability to read so well, and occasionally made the child write a few sentences in the letter to her grandmother to show off her fine handwriting. Finally, one Christmas, to flesh out the image of the child she had been building up over the years, she took most of the rat-cut coffee money and took the child to the nearest big town to have her photograph taken in a professional studio.

It was a posed, stilted photograph in a style that went out of fashion thirty years before. The child was dressed in a frilly white dress trimmed with ribbons, much too long for her age. She wore long white nylon socks and white T-strap shoes. Her hair was done in perfect drop curls, with a part to the side and two front curls caught up with a large white bow. In the photograph she stood quite straight with her feet together and her right hand stiffly bent to touch an artificial rose in a vase on a rattan table beside her. She did not smile.

Her grandparents who were the recipients of a large framed print on matte paper saw a dark-skinned child with long dark hair, a straight nose, and enormous, very serious eyes. Despite the fancy clothes, everything about her had a countrified air except for the penetrating eyes which had none of the softness and shyness of country children. Miss Christie was a little embarrassed by this gift, and hid the picture in her bureau drawer for it had none of the gloss of the photos of her children and grandchildren which stood on her bureau. But she could not put the picture away entirely; something about the child haunted her and she constantly looked at it to see what in this child was of her flesh and blood. The child had her father's weak mouth, it seemed, though the defiant chin and the bold eyes undoubtedly came from her mother. Maybe it was the serious, steady, unchildlike gaze that caused Miss Christie sometimes to look at the pictue for minutes at a time as if it mesmerised her. Then she would get hold of herself again and angrily put the picture back into the drawer.

Despite her better judgement, Miss Christie found herself intensely curious about this child whose mother made her into such a little paragon and whose eyes gazed out at the world so directly.

Soon, she broached the subject obliquely to her husband. One evening at dusk as the two of them sat on the verandah, she said, "Well, just look at the two of us. Look how many children and grandchildren we have, and not a one to keep our company".

"Hm. So life stay. Once your children go to town, country too lonely for them after that."

"I suppose so. But it really would be nice to have a young person about the house again." They dropped the subject then, but she kept bringing it up from time to time.

Finally she said, as if thinking about it for the first time, "But Dolphie, why don't we get Myrtle's little girl here?"

"What! And rake up that old thing again? You must be mad."

"But nobody has to know who she is."

"Then you dont know how ol'nayga fas'. They bound to find out."

"Well, they can't prove anything. She doesn't have our name. She bears her mother's name."

They argued about it on and off for weeks, then finally they decided to invite the child to stay for a week or two.

When Laura came, she was overawed by the big house, the patrician old couple who were always so clean and sweet-smelling as if perpetually laundered each day anew by Mirie the cook. She fell even more silent, speaking only when spoken to, and then in a low voice which could hardly be heard.

Miss Christie was gratified that she was so much lighter than the photograph (indeed, Myrtle had quarrelled with the photographer for just this reason) and although she was exactly like a country mouse, she did fill the house with her presence. Already Miss Christie was busy planning the child's future, getting her into decent clothes, correcting her speech, erasing her country accent, teaching her table manners, getting her to take a complete bath every day – a fact which was so novel to the child who came from a place where everyone bathed in a bath pan once a week since the water had to be carried on their heads one mile uphill from the spring.

In the child Miss Christie saw a lump of clay which held every promise of being moulded into something satisfactory. The same energy with which Miss Christie entered into a 'good' marriage, successfully raised six children and saw that they made good marriages themselves, that impelled her to organise the Mothers Union and the School Board – that energy was now to be expended on this latest product which relatives in the know referred to as 'Bertram's stray shot'.

Although her husband fussed and fumed, he too liked the idea of having a child in the house once more though he thought her a funny little thing who hardly made a sound all day, unlike the boisterous family they had reared. And so, as if in a dream, the child found herself permanently transported from her mother's two-room house to this mansion of her father's.

Of course her father was never mentioned and she only knew it was him from the photograph because he had signed it. She gazed often at this photograph, trying to transmute it into a being of flesh and blood from which she had been created, but failed utterly. In fact, she was quite unable to deduce even the smallest facet of his character from the picture. All that she saw was a smiling face that in some indefinable way looked like all the faces in the other photographs. All were bland and sweet. In none of these faces were there lines, or frowns, or blemishes, or marks of ugliness such as a squint eye, or a broken nose, or kinky hair, or big ears, or broken teeth which afflicted all the other people she had known. Faced with such perfection, she ceased to look at herself in the mirror.

She had gone to live there during the summer holidays and Miss Christie took every opportunity to add polish to her protegé whom she introduced everywhere as 'my little adopted'. As part of the child's education, Miss Christie taught her to polish mahogany furniture and to bake cakes, to polish silver and clean panes of glass, all of which objects had been foreign to the child's former upbringing.

The child liked to remain inside the house which was cool and dark and shaded for outside, with its huge treeless lawn and beyond, the endless pastures, frightened her.

She had grown up in a part of the mountain cockpits where a gravel road was the only thing that broke the monotony of the humpbacked hills and endless hills everywhere. There were so many hills that for half of the day their house and yard were damp and dark and moss grew on the sides of the clay path. It was only at midday when the sun was directly overhead that they received light. The houses were perched precariously up the hillsides with slippery paths leading to them from the road, and if anyone bothered to climb to the tops of the hills, all they would see was more mountains. Because it was so hilly the area seemed constantly to be in a dark blue haze, broken only by the occasional hibiscus or croton and the streams of brightly colour-ed birds dashing through the foliage. They were hemmed in by the mountains on all sides and Laura liked it, because all her life was spent in space that was enclosed and finite, protecting her from what dangers she did not even know.

And then, from the moment she had journeyed to the railway station some ten miles away and got on to the train and it had begun to travel through the endless canefields, she had begun to feel afraid. For suddenly the skies had opened up so wide all around her; the sun beat down and there was the endless noisy clacking of the train wheels. She felt naked and anxious, as if suddenly exposed, and there was nowhere to hide.

When she got off the train at the other end, there were no canefields there, but the land was still flat and open, for this was all rolling pastureland. Her curiosity about the herds of cattle she saw grazing in the shade of an occasional tree could not diminish the fear she felt at being so exposed.

Her father's parents' house was set on the top of a hill from where they could see for miles in all directions. Whenever she went outside she felt dizzy for the sky was so wide it was like being enclosed within a huge blue bowl. The summer was cloudless. And the hills were so far away they were lost in blue. But then summer came to an end and it was time for her to go

45

to school. The nearest school was three miles away. Her grand-mother, deciding that this was too far for her to walk – though walking greater distances had meant nothing in her former life – had arranged for her to travel to and from school on the bus which went by at the right time each day. This single fact impressed her most as showing the power and might of her grandmother.

She was glad of the bus for she did not want to walk alone to school. Now the clear summer days were ending, the clouds had begun to gather in the sky, fat cumulus clouds that travelled in packs and in this strange and empty country became ugly and menacing. They reminded her of the pictures she used to get in Sunday School showing Jesus coming to earth again, floating down on one of these fat white clouds. And because the Jesus of their church was a man who had come to judge and punish sinners, these pictures only served to remind her that she was a sinner and that God would one day soon appear out of the sky flashing fire and brimstone to judge and condemn her. And until he came, the clouds were there to watch her. For why else did they move, change themselves, assume shapes of creatures awesome and frightful, if not to torment her with her un-worthiness? Sometimes when she stood on the barbecue and looked back at the house outlined against the sky, the house itself seemed to move and she would feel a wave of dizziness as if the whole earth was moving away off course and leaving her standing there alone in the emptiness.

She would run quickly inside and find Miss Christie or Mirie or somebody. As long as it was another human being to share the world with.

While all day long she would feel a vague longing for her mother and brothers and all the people she had known since childhood, she never felt lonely, for if her mother had given her nothing else, in taking her out of one life without guaranteeing her placement in the next, she had unwittingly raised her for a life of solitude. Here in this big house she wandered from room to room and said nothing all day, for now her lips were sealed from shyness. To her newly sensitised ears, her words came out flat and unmusical and she would look with guilt at the photographs and silently beg pardon for being there.

There were no other children around the house and she was now so physically removed from others that she had no chance to meet anyone. Sometimes she would walk down the driveway to the tall black gate hoping that some child would pass along and talk so that they could be friends, but whenever anyone happened by, her shyness would cause her to hide behind the stone pillar so they would not see her. And although her grandmother said nothing on the subject, she instinctively knew after a while that she would never in this place find anyone good enough to bring into Miss Christie's house.

Although she liked the feeling of importance it gave her to get on and off the bus at the school gate – the only child to do so – most times she watched with envy the other children walking home from school, playing, yelling, and rolling in the road. They wore no shoes and she envied them this freedom, for her feet, once free like theirs except for Sundays, were now encased in socks and patent leather shoes handed down from one or the other of the rightful grandchildren who lived in Kingston or New York.

Most days the bus was on time. Every morning she would wait by the tall black gate for the bus to arrive. The bus would arrive on time every day. Except Thursday. Sometimes on Thursdays the bus wouldn't arrive until late evening. She would nevertheless every Thursday go to the gates and wait, knowing in her heart that the bus would not come. Miss Christie would sometimes walk out and stand by the gate and look the road up and down.

Sometimes Mass Dolphie passing on his way from one pasture to the next would rein in his horse and would also stand by the gate and look up the road. All three would stand silently. The road swayed white in an empty world. The silence hummed like telegraph wires. Her life hung in the air waiting on a word from Miss Christie. Her chest began to swell like a balloon getting bigger and bigger. "The bus isn't coming. You'll have to walk," Miss Christie pronounced with finality.

47

"Oh Miss Christie, just a few minutes more," she begged. It was the only thing she begged for. But she knew that the bus wouldn't come, and now, at this terribly late hour, she would have to walk alone the three miles to school in a world that was empty of people. She would walk very fast, the dust of the marl road swirling round her ankles, along this lonely road that curved past the graveyard. Above, following every step of the way, the fat clouds sat smirking and smug in the pale blue sky. She hated them for all they knew about her. Her clumsiness, her awkwardness, the fact that she did not belong in this light and splendid place. They sat there in judgement on her every Thursday. Thursday, the day before market day. The day of her Armageddon.

Thursdays the old bus would sit on the road miles above, packed with higglers and their crocus bags, bankras and chickens. The bus would start right enough: somewhere on the road above the bus would start in the dawn hours, full and happy. And then, a few miles after, the bus would gently shudder and like a torn metal bird would ease to a halt with a cough and a sigh and settle down on the road, too tired and worn out to move. It would remain there until evening, the market women sitting in the shade and fanning the flies away with the men importantly gathered around the machine, arguing and cursing until evening when the earth was cool again and the driver would go slowly, everything patched up till next Thursday when the higglers descended with their crocus bags and their bankras, their laughter and their girth and their quarrelling and their ferocious energy which would prove too much for the old bus. Then with a sigh it would again lie still on the road above her. Every Thursday.

Sometimes though if she managed to dawdle long enough Miss Christie would say, "Heavens, It's 10 o'clock. You can't go to school again".

'O Miss Christie' she would cry silently 'thank you, thank you'.

Sometimes when she didn't go to school Mass Dolphie would

let her dig around in his irish potato patch collecting the tiny potatoes for herself.

Digging potatoes was safe. She could not see the sky. And she never knew when a really big potato would turn up among all the tiny ones.

"Like catching fish, eh?" Mass Dolphie said and she agreed though she didn't know how that was having never seen the sea. But she would laugh too.

II

One day they got a letter from the child's father. He was coming home with his wife on a visit. It wasn't long after their initial joy at hearing the news that the grandparents realised that difficulties were bound to arise with the child. For one thing, they hadn't told their son about her, being a little ashamed that they had not consulted him at all before coming to the decision to take her. Besides, it was a little awkward to write to him about such matters at his home, since from all they had heard of American women they believed that there was a strong possibility that his wife would open his letters.

Their immediate decision was to send the child home, but that too presented certain problems since it was still during the school term and they couldn't quite make up their minds what they would tell her mother to explain a change of heart. They certainly couldn't tell her the truth for even to them the truth seemed absurd: that they wanted to return the little girl because her father was coming. For once, Miss Christie was at a loss. It was Mr Dolphie who took a firm line. "Write and ask him what to do," he instructed his wife, "after all, its his child. If he doesn't want her here when he comes then he can tell us what we should do with her".

They were suprised but not overly so when their son wrote

that they should do nothing about the child as he would be greatly amused to see her.

Mr Dolphie didn't see any cause for amusement in the situation and thought that it was just like his youngest son to take a serious thing and make a joke of it and all in all act in a reckless and irresponsible manner. He had certainly hoped that Bertram had finally settled down to the seriousness of life.

Long before they told the child the news of her father's coming, she knew, for without deliberately listening to their conversations, she seemed to absorb and intuitively understand everything that happened in the house.

Since hearing the news there had been a joy in her heart, for her mother had told her so often that one day this mysterious father of hers would come and claim her as his own that she had grown to believe it. She knew that he would come and rescue her from fears as tenuous as clouds and provide her with nothing but bright Thursdays.

But when she searched out the photograph from the ones on the bureau, his face held that unreadable, bland smile and his eyes gave off nothing that would show her just how he intended to present his love for her.

One day Miss Christie said to her, "Laura, our son is coming on a visit. Mr Bertram". She said it as if the child and the man bore no relationship to each other. "He is coming with his wife. We haven't seen him for so many years".

Yes. Since I was born, Laura thought.

"Now Laura, I except you to be on your best behaviour when they are here."

"Yes mam."

Laura showed no emotion at all as Miss Christie continued to chat on the subject. How does one behave with a father? Laura thought. She had no experience of this. There were so few fathers among all the people she knew.

Miss Christie turned the house upside down in a frenzy of preparation for her son's visit. Without being told so, Laura understood that such preparation was not so much for the son as for his white wife. She was quite right, for as Miss Christie told Mirie, "these foreign women are really too fresh, you know. Half of them don't really come from anywhere but they believe that everybody from Jamaica is a monkey and live in trees. I am really glad my son is bringing her here so that she can see how we live". Laura silently assented to that, for who in the wide world could keep up a life that was as spotless and well ordered as Miss Christie's?

Laura longed to talk to somebody about her father. To find out what he was really like. But she did not want to ask Miss Christie. She thought of writing secretly to her mother and telling her that Mr Bertram was coming, asking what he was really like, but she was too timid to do anything behind Miss Christie's back for Miss Christie was so all-knowing she was bound to find out. Sometimes she wanted to ask Mirie the cook who had been working with the family for nearly forty years. But although she got into the habit of dropping into the roomy kitchen and sitting at the table there for hours, she never got up the nerve to address Mirie, and Mirie, a silent and morose woman, never addressed her at all. She believed, though, that Mirie liked her, for frequently, without saying a word, she would give her some tidbit from the pot, or a sample of the cookies, or bread and guava jelly, though she knew that Miss Christie did not approve of eating between meals. But apart from grunting every now and then as she went about her tasks, Mirie said nothing at all on the subject of Mr Bertram or any other being. Laura wished that Mirie would talk to her, for she found the kitchen the most comforting part of the house.

Her father and his wife arrived one day when she was at school. When she got home, she was too shy to go in, and was hanging around trying to hide behind a post when Miss Christie spotted her.

"Oh Laura, come and meet my son," said Miss Christie and swept her into the living room. "Mina," she said to a yellow-haired woman sitting there, "this is Laura, the little adopted I was telling you about". Laura first vaguely made out the woman, then Mass Dolphie, then a strange man in the shadows, but she was too shy to give him more than a covert glance. He did not address her but gave a smile which barely moved his lips. In days to come she would get accustomed to that smile, which was not as bland as in the photograph. To his daughter, he paid no more attention. It was his wife who fussed over the little girl, asking questions and exclaiming over her curls. Laura could hardly understand anything the woman said, but was impressed at how trim and neat she was, at the endless fascination of her clothes, her jewellery, her laughter, her accent, her perfume, her assurance. Looking at her long polished nails, Laura had a picture of her mother's hands, the nails cracked and broken like a man's from her work in the fields; of her mother's dark face, her coarse shrill voice. And she was bitterly ashamed. Knowing the mother she had come from, it was no wonder, she thought, that her father could not acknowledge her.

She was extremely uneasy with the guests in the house. Their presence strained to the fullest the new social graces that Miss Christie had inculcated in her. Now she had a two-fold anxiety: not to let her mother down to Miss Christie, and not to let Miss Christie down in front of this white woman from the United States of America.

For all the woman's attentions, it was the man that she wanted to attend her, acknowledge her, love her. But he never did. She contrived at all times to be near him, to sit in his line of vision, to 'accidentally' appear on the path when he went walking through the pastures. The man did not see her. He loved to talk, his voice going on and on in a low rumble like the waves of the sea she had never seen, the ash on his cigarette getting longer till it fell on his clothes or Miss Christie's highly polished floor. But he never talked to her. This caused her even greater anxiety than Miss Christie's efforts at 'polishing' her, for while she felt that Miss Christie was trying, however painful it was, to build her up, she could not help feeling that her father's indifference did nothing so much as to reduce her, nullify her. Laura would have wondered if he knew who she was if she hadn't known that Miss Christie had written to him on the subject. She decided then that all his indifference was merely part of a play, that he wanted to surprise her when he did claim her, and was working up to one magical moment of recognition that would thereafter illuminate both their lives forever and ever. In the daytime that is how she consoled herself but at nights she cried in the little room where she slept alone in the fearful shadow of the breadfruit tree against the window pane.

Then Thursday came round again and in this anxiety she even forgot about her father. As usual the bus was late and Laura hung around the gate hoping that Miss Christie would forget she was there until it was too late to walk to school. The road curved white and lonely in the empty morning, silent save for the humming of bees and the beating of her own heart. Then Miss Christie and Mina appeared on the verandah and obviously saw her. Talking together, they started to walk slowly towards the gate where she stood, trapped by several impulses. Laura's heart beat faster then almost stopped as her father appeared from the orange grove and approached the two women. Now the three of them were walking towards her. They were now near enough for Laura to hear what they were saying but her eyes were only on her father.

"Oh dear, that old bus. Laura is going to be late again," Miss Christie said.

"Oh for chrissake. Why don't you stop fussing so much about the bloody little bastard," her son shouted.

Laura heard no more for after one long moment when her heart somersaulted once there was no time for hearing anything else for her feet of their own volition had set off at a run down the road and by the time she got to the school gates she had made herself an orphan and there were no more clouds.

Real Old Time T'ing

Is the one name Patricia did start up bout how Papa Sterling
need a new house for it look bad how their father living in this
old board house it dont even have sanitary convenience. Sanitary convenience! So it dont name bath house any more? Then if
she so hot on sanitary convenience why she down here a buy up
all the old water goblet and china basin she can find a talk say is
real country this and how she just finding her roots.

Anyway she nuh Papa Sterling big girl the one that did marry
the lawyer fellow from Kingston that always get him name in
Gleaner. Big big lawyer. Name Akeson. But we wont go into all
the ups and downs she did have in her life before that piece of
luck drop into her lap. And is luck fe true mi dear. The guy
have money and he drive big car and he good looking caan
done.

Let me tell you not a thing was wrong with Papa Sterling
house except that it did need a little fixing up here and there.
True, he getting on and he could do with a little more comfort
in him old age and since Miss Mae die he really dont keep the
place up like how she did keep it nice. But what yu expect? Nuh
the one-eye Doris he still have a look after him and she so busy
dropping pickney year after year that what she know bout
keeping house could write on postage stamp. But nothing really
wrong with the house for them to go on so. After all is the very
same house them all birth and grow up in and anything wrong
with them?

But hear the one Patricia she – this is one Sunday she did
drive down with the pickney dem. The husband didnt come:

"Poppa, this place is really just too bad. The children shame
to come here. We have to do something about it."

54

dont know if I would spend all my life in foreign and get accent like Miss Myrtella and then end up back down in these backward parts, but every dog have him bone.

See here, this Miss Myrtella cause one excitement when she come. Nuh mini-bus she one did take from Kingston to bring down all her things! From she land up in the place news bout her spread. First of all although Miss Myrtella is a hard-back woman by now she still slim like a young girl and she talk in a little-little voice like she caan mash ants. Any time yu see her, day or night, she look like she just step out of fashion magazine. She have bout six wig in all kind of colour – every one of them full up with curl. When she put on one of her wig and her cheeks rouge up and her lipstick and her London frock with the way-out style and her high-heel shoes, see here man, is a good thing is not much traffic to stop for collision would bound to occur.

Them idlers playing domino used to laugh at Miss Myrtella for her curly curly hair and her foreign ways and the way she talk funny. But since from she arrive in the district she start drop money yu should see how their tune change.

Miss Myrtella is Papa Sterling cousin, far remove, bout third cousin. Mek me see, Papa Sterling grandfather Mass Jake did have a daughter on the side with a Fletcher woman name Addie. This now is before she marry her husband Leabert Mason. And this daughter was just a young little thing when she fall for one of them Parks boy the same bad lot of them from Rocky Mountain and Miss Myrtella is their daughter. Is not her real father the Parks boy that did send for her to England but is her step-father. Him was a PWD man name Austin Phelps that did come down here one time they was building bridge and fall in love with her mother.

So because Papa Sterling was the only family she have left bout these parts Miss Myrtella did lean very heavy pon him from the start. This time you know, Miss Mae just dead and Papa still depress like.

Miss Myrtella would dress to back foot in the middle of the day and march up to Papa house.

"Ho Cousin Orris," she call out. Horace is Papa Sterling first name. "Oi dont know wot to do hit his so howful to be ha woman holl holone hin this worl Cousin Orris."

Is same way she talk with her mouth curl round the words. And she there in her high heel shoes and fanning her face and shaking her curls. Then she would complain bout some little thing that gone wrong at her yard that any other woman round here would fix themself without worrying the man dem. But not Miss Myrtella.

"Cousin Orris," she always saying, "Can you please come? You will know hexactly wot to do".

So Papa Sterling would please no puss and follow her down to her yard, squaring his shoulder all the way and practically rolling up him sleeve to help out poor little Miss Myrtella.

Now you understand why everybody always asking Papa how the courtship coming. To tell the truth I dont think no courtship was going on or that Papa had anything serious on him mind. After Miss Mae death we all use to encourage him to get married again and he would shake him head and say, "Ah no, sister. Woman confine. Woman confine". So we take that to mean that Papa enjoying him freedom and woman too confining.

Then one day the one Patricia no arrive from town. And right behind her nuh truck full with board and cement, steel and paint pan. The truck pull right into Papa Sterling yard and they start unload.

Patricia step out of her car and run up to where Papa there scratching him head and thinking is mistake.

"O Poppa, I am so excited. At last we are going to start on the house. Poppa I write to every one of the children and tell them they must contribute.

"We get the money for the house from all of them except that wutless Edgar. Poppa I am going to fix up the house beautiful for you. I even buy the kitchen curtain already since sale was on.

"Leslie promise to give you his old living room things since his wife buying a new set and Mary say she shipping her old stove for she get a new one too. Poppa, we buying everything special for the house it cost the earth but Ken and me who bearing the brunt of it decide that nothing is too good for Poppa."

All this time Papa still have him mouth open for he is a man not use to people a tell him what they going to do to his property.

But when Patricia start talk she really not paying no mine to anybody else. So she dont notice how Papa take the news. She run off gone to boss the truck man dem doing the unloading.

This is just the start. More truck come with things for Papa house. Mass Ersie get contract to do the building. Brother Samson get contract fe build the new tank. Mass P get contract fe the roof. Cephas get contract to paint it. Obadiah get contract to level and gravel the driveway. Even Son-Son the electrician get contract to run wire for Patricia say she sure government soon send light down there.

Patricia in and out all day long till you would think is down here she live now. We all wonder if her husband and children dont need her.

From she meet Miss Myrtella Patricia dislike her for now she see she is not the only one in the district can wear good clothes and know bout green tea and sticking out her little finger when she drinking out of cup. Beside, Miss Myrtella did live most of her life in foreign and that is one thing that Patricia never do.

Patricia always there passing word bout Miss Myrtella, how she have to wear wig because her real hair so picky-picky. How she dont have no class. How she cant speak properly. How her clothes too young for her. How she go on like she cant mash ants and always bothering her father about some foolishness or other. But she still sweet to Miss Myrtella face.

So one day Miss Myrtella invite Patricia to tea. When she say tea is not bissie or chocolate she talking bout. Is real green tea mi dear. Just like them English woman.

Of course Patricia rush to say yes. She dying to see inside Miss Myrtella house. Patricia always rushing to see inside people house ever since she decide say she finding her roots.

One day she down here and hear that Miss Miriam sick. She rush take soup for Miss Miriam. She look Miss Miriam little two-bi-four house up and down and she see Miss Miriam have some old bruck-down chair stick up in the roof. She swear same time that she need two bruck-down chair just like that and pay Miriam five dollar for them. When she gone Miriam laugh like goat and feel better right away. She was just getting ready to throw weh the chair for Cephas promise to fix them from the devil was a boy and she still a wait.

Then another time Patricia go walk up the hill past Miss Icy yard. She see Miss Icy old Calidonia stove throw out in the yard. It been there from the year one when Miss Icy get kerosene stove so till junjo all take it up.

Hear the Patricia she:

"Oh my, a real Calidonia Dover! Oh Miss Icy you dont know how I love and appreciate these old things. They remind me of my happy childhood. And you have them just throw weh out a door. I would do anything to get a stove like that."

You ever hear anything like that bout happy childhood? As if she couldn't wait to turn her tail on the place. But with one thing and another she manage to get inside Miss Icy house. She just love Miss Icy water cooler! She just adore her 'Panish jar!

Miss Icy hem and haw but she finally agree to sell Patricia whole heap of her things, even some old spoon and plate and other carouches she have from long time. Miss Icy so glad for she thirty dollars richer.

And let me say here and now that no matter what you say about the one Patricia, and you can say plenty, she never try to get something for nothing. She always willing to pay. In fact this vex some people sometime for she think money can buy everything.

Anway, after that everybody get ready for the Miss Patricia she.

As soon as she arrive everybody start tell her how their dear old mother die and leave them this old goblet or that old chamber pot. Patricia so greedy she want everything, as long as is old time ting.

She will beg. She will plead. She will offer more money. They refuse. She keep offering more and more for she cant bear to do without anything she set her heart on. So the price she paying getting higher and higher and the poeple glad to get rid of all the ol'bruck furniture they have around. They want to go and trust plastic living room chair and aluminium dinette set down at Mr V. Store. Everybody a laugh and say Patricia must be opening junk yard a Kingston.

So when she tell Miss Myrtella yes she will come to tea is really because she want to see what ol'bruck in Miss Myrtella house she can get to buy.

And is true for the minute she walk inside Miss Myrtella house her eye start popping for is pure old time ting Miss Myrtella house full up with. Patricia start tremble she so excite-up. Is like she still little girl and Christmas just come.

She walking up and down in Miss Myrtella house as if she daze.

"Oh Miss M. I just must have this little brown milk jug. It is the spitting image of a sugar bowl I have. O Miss Myrtella, a commode! And a bentwood rocker! A Coronation mug! Cut glass punch bowl! Pie crust side table! Claw foot umbrella rack! Wicker flower planter! Four poster bed! Another four poster bed! O Miss Myrtella, I dont know where to start. I must have this little milk jug. How much you will take for it?"

Miss Myrtella just following her from room to room smiling her little smile and not saying a word.

So after a time it probably reach even thick skin Patricia brain that Miss M not saying yea or nay to any of her offer. So finally she say to Miss Myrtella:

"What a beautiful little decanter. How much you want for it? My friends will be so envious when they come to my house and see it."

Miss Myrtella never say a word but she take the decanter out of Patricia hand and put it back on the what-not where it belong.

"Ho Miss Patricia. That was my very mother hown. Is her grand mother did give er and she give me. So you see his very

61

hold. Oi om so hafraid you break hit. Hit his my greatest treasure."

"But Miss Myrtella, there is nobody in these country parts to admire it. I will make you a good offer."

"Ho, Miss Patricia. Tea his served."

The tea just aggravate Patricia for everything Miss Myrtella using is old time ting. And Miss Myrtella rubbing salt in the wound by telling her how this one did belong to her mother and this one to her grandmother and this was a wedding present and this was an anniversary present from her late husband. And Patricia vex how she never have nobody to die and leave her old time ting.

But Patricia dont give up so easy. As soon as she done the tea so braps, she start walk up and down Miss Myrtella house again a fingle up her things and telling her how much she will pay.

"Ho, oi om well heware of the value of my treasures. Oi use to visit hantique shops hin Hengland you know." Miss Myrtella tell her. "But oi dont put a price hon these things, they or my treasures."

"But Miss Myrtella," Patricia burst out, for she not listening to a word. "You no mus want get rid of some of this junk. They make the place so chuck-up there is hardly anywhere to walk."

"Miss Patricia," Miss Myrtella say, and she still a smile though her little voice get hard," You seem to forget that this his my ouse. Hit his not ha store you know."

"Well!" is all Patricia could get out she so vex. She never have anybody round here talk to her like that before.

"Well! If you want to insult the very guest you invite to your house for tea I can see you have no breeding." And with that Patricia grab up her handbag and flounce out of the house.

And from that day she hate Miss Myrtella with a living hatred.

But she console herself that when Papa new house finish she would throw a big house opening party and invite everybody who is anybody in the district to come and admire the house. Myrtella would get invite over her dead body.

So now Papa new house getting bigger and bigger. All day

long the men round busy mixing cement, a lay tile, a paint. The whole time Papa up and down a joke with the workmen. He looking at everything going on but is like none of it dont have anything to do with him and he wondering where the pretty little board house he build with his own two hands gone to.

And I notice that as the new house getting bigger and bigger Papa like he getting squeeze smaller and smaller and he spending less and less time there. Is not really me that notice it in truth. Is Puncie pinch me one day and ask me if me dont notice how Papa spending so much time down at Miss Myrtella yard.

Well up to then I never give it any real thought. I just did figure that Papa looking for a little peace and quiet, for he cant find none at his yard.

"No. Is more than that man," say the Puncie she. "Is really courting him courting".

"Then is how you know that Puncie?"

"Ah," is all Puncie willing to say.

Puncie just like radio for as fast as she get anything she take it and broadcast it. So right away everybody know something going on in truth between Papa and Miss Myrtella.

But the strange thing is that not a soul tease Papa or say a word about it. Everybody just pretend they dont know what going on though they watching every move. And is like everybody in the district holding their breath. They dont want Patricia to get to know bout it for she really vex with Miss Myrtella and if she ever hear bout the courting she bound to try and mash it up. And everybody round here really love Papa and would like to see him happy. And we getting to love Miss Myrtella too for once you get use to her speaky-spoky ways you find out that she have a heart of gold inside.

And these days Papa he walking straight all the time and stepping high like young boy and he cant keep a little smile from his mouth corner the whole time. As for Miss M, she there fluttering up and down like butterfly and every week she gone town to buy new clothes.

Then Cephas no tell me that Papa order one new suit from

Tailor Vincent. He say is for the house opening but I really wonder if is the house opening he so concern about.

So things go on like this for a few more week. The excitement soon done for the house almost finish.

Patricia planning a big cook-up. Plenty of Papa children coming specially from abroad. Patricia invite everybody who is anybody in the district. Except Miss Myrtella. Papa know but he dont say a thing. And we wonder what going to happen.

The party was on the Sunday and the Saturday before, early in the morning, Mark Hanson nuh drive up to Papa yard in him taxi and me see Papa rush out of the house and jump into it. Mrs Hanson also in the car. The car drive off before you could say kemps. Where Papa gone so early in the morning wearing him new suit? Dont is tomorrow him suppose to be wearing that suit?

The taxi dont come back till dark. Patricia busy a organise everything for if is one thing you can say bout her she really work hard. But she still find time to quarrel how Papa leave her with all the work and dont even say a word to her. But is not so much the work as is vex she vex how Papa dont tell her his business.

Then Puncie no come to mi house that evening so tell me that the taxi did stop to pick up Miss Myrtella who dress to back foot in hat and all. Puncie did take fas the evening go to Mr Hanson yard to try find out where he did take the two of them dress up so and why, but Mr Hanson wouldn't let a thing drop.

By now I did have a pretty good idea but I dont say a word, for I believe all kind of truth will come to light at the house opening party and it wont be to Patricia liking.

Anyway the party day finally arrive and I dont have word to describe how everything nice. Everybody dress up in their Sunday best and come. Everybody but Miss Myrtella for she dont get invite.

Well I couldn't begin to describe the food. I will just say it good and plentiful caan done. Ol'naygah never stuff themself so as on that day and pickney them eat cake and ice cream so till them all have nightmare the night. But that was later.

64

Plenty people jump up give speech. Parson come bless the house. Even Parson wife was there. Count Libby and his Mento Band was in attendance all the way from Hanover.

And hear this! Now I come to the best part of everything. The big surprise of the evening. It happen when Papa get up to turn thanks to everybody.

Papa and all the other important people sitting at a long table on the verandah with them back to the house. The rest of we sitting down at some table outside in the yard (and is truck did bring the table down from Kingston special, mi dear).

Anyway Papa launch into him speech. And we all settle down to laugh for Papa is well known for him speechifying. Then finally now, Papa winding up him speech, you can see that. Him start thank Patricia and all the children for their kindness in building him this lovely house.

"My children have made me proud of them tonight. A can stand up in front of mi neighbour and friend dem and say, look at what my children have done for me. This magnificent and grandiloquent edifice here will stand as a living testimonial to their love of a father."

Then him sort of stop and look behind him back to the door mouth. Somebody inside – I find out afterwards is Mrs Hanson – give him a signal.

Then Papa Sterling say: "But friends, you all know that a house is not a home without a woman".

Everybody cheer.

"And not just any woman."

"Thats right."

"True word sah."

"Amen."

"And since I myself turn old man now, is a real old time ting I need to keep me warm."

Everybody laugh.

"And so my friends I want to make an announcement."

Eh-eh. Everybody start whispering and look at their neighbour.

"Friends, I have found a lady to share this house with."

"Everybody start bawl out, "What, Papa!"

"Yes, friends. Is a lady well known to all of you."

This time everybody start whisper and carry on so much they hardly hear the rest of what he saying.

"My friends, I want to tell you that yesterday that lovely lady Mistress Myrtella Lee and I got..."

But we never wait to hear the end of it. See here, the house nearly pop down. People start to whistle and shout and cheer and stomp them foot and jump up and down and throw them hat in the air. The mento band strike up and nobody notice that every jack man strike up a different tune.

For Mrs Hanson nuh coming out of the house. And who she leading by the hand but Miss Myrtella. Miss Myrtella dress in lavender from head to foot – lavender dress, lavender hat, lavender shoes, lavender lipstick, lavender nail polish and lavender handbag. She smiling and smiling just like a young bride. Me tell you, the woman looking so beautiful I feel that I just want to cry.

Everybody start crowd round Papa and Miss Myrtella a shake them hand and kiss them. Even Papa children joining in though you can see that still and for all that they looking surprise caan done.

So then I start to look at the one Patricia. Patricia there a stand with her mouth open like she catching fly. She just cant believe it. She looking so vex I believe she would mash up the place. But then she look round and her expression change for she see how everybody else so glad about the news. And right away I see her brain start to work and she come forward and kiss her father.

Then she kiss Miss Myrtella. She dont say a word to her. But she kiss her.

But I know that everything is going to be alright. Patricia not going to make no fuss. She going to swallow her pride. For I know how her brain work. And I sure she thinking say that now Miss Myrtella is her step-mother she have somebody to die and leave her all kind of old time ting.

Do Angels Wear Brassieres?

BECCKA down on her knees ending her goodnight prayers and Cherry telling her softly, "And Ask God to bless Auntie Mary." Beccka vex that anybody could interrupt her private conversation with God so, say loud loud, "No. Not praying for nobody that tek weh mi best glassy eye marble".

"Beccka!" Cherry almost crying in shame, "Shhhhh! She wi hear you. Anyway she did tell you not to roll them on the floor when she have her headache."

"A hear her already" – this is the righteous voice of Auntie Mary in the next room – "But I am sure that God is not listening to the like of she. Blasphemous little wretch".

She add the last part under her breath and with much lifting of her eyes to heaven she turn back to her nightly reading of the Imitations of Christ.

"Oooh Beccka, Rebecca, see what yu do," Cherry whispering, crying in her voice.

Beccka just stick out her tongue at the world, wink at God who she know right now in the shape of a big fat anansi in a corner of the roof, kiss her mother and get into bed.

As soon as her mother gone into Auntie Mary room to try make it up and the whole night come down with whispering, Beccka whip the flash light from off the dressing table and settle down under the blanket to read. Beccka reading the Bible in secret from cover to cover not from any conviction the little wretch but because everybody round her always quoting that book and Beccka want to try and find flaw and question she can best them with.

Next morning Auntie Mary still vex. Auntie Mary out by the tank washing clothes and slapping them hard on the big rock. Fat sly-eye Katie from the next yard visiting and consoling her. Everybody visiting Auntie Mary these days and consoling her for the crosses she have to bear (that is Beccka they talking about). Fat Katie have a lot of time to walk bout consoling because ever since hard time catch her son and him wife a town they come country to cotch with Katie. And from the girl walk through the door so braps! Katie claim she too sickly to do any washing or housework. So while the daughter-in-law beating suds at her yard she over by Auntie Mary washpan say she keeping her company. Right now she consoling about Beccka who (as she telling Auntie Mary) every decent-living upright Christian soul who is everybody round here except that Dorcas Waite about whom one should not dirty one's mouth to talk yes every clean living person heart go out to Auntie Mary for with all due respect to a sweet mannersable child like Cherry her daughter is the devil own pickney. Not that anybody saying a word about Cherry God know she have enough trouble on her head from she meet up that big hard back man though young little gal like that never shoulda have business with no married man. Katie take a breath long enough to ask question:

"But see here Miss Mary you no think Cherry buck up the devil own self when she carrying her? Plenty time that happen you know. Remember that woman over Allside that born the pickney with two head praise Jesus it did born dead. But see here you did know one day she was going down river to wash clothes and is the devil own self she meet. Yes'm. Standing right there in her way. She pop one big bawling before she faint weh and when everybody run come not a soul see him. Is gone he gone. But you no know where he did gone? No right inside that gal. Right inna her belly. And Miss Mary I telling you the living truth, just as the baby borning the midwife no see a shadow fly out of the mother and go right cross the room. She frighten so till she close her two eye tight and is so the devil escape."

"Well I dont know about that. Beccka certainly dont born

with no two head or nothing wrong with her. Is just hard ears she hard ears."

"Den no so me saying?"

"The trouble is, Cherry is too soft to manage her. As you look hard at Cherry herself she start cry. She was never a strong child and she not a strong woman, her heart just too soft."

"All the same right is right and there is only one right way to bring up a child and that is by bus' ass pardon my french Miss Mary but hard things call for hard words. That child should be getting blows from the day she born. Then she wouldn't be so force-ripe now. Who cant hear must feel for the rod and reproof bring wisdom but a child left to himself bringeth his mother to shame. Shame, Miss Mary."

"Is true. And you know I wouldn't mind if she did only get into mischief Miss Katie but what really hurt me is how the child know so much and show off. Little children have no right to have so many things in their brain. Guess what she ask me the other day nuh? – if me know how worms reproduce."

"Say what, maam?"

"As Jesus is me judge. Me big woman she come and ask that. Reproduce I say. Yes Auntie Mary she say as if I stupid. When the man worm and the lady worm come together and they have baby. You know how it happen? – Is so she ask me."

"What you saying maam? Jesus of Nazareth!"

"Yes, please. That is what the child ask me. Lightning come strike me dead if is lie I lie. In my own house. My own sister pickney. So help me I was so frighten that pickney could so impertinent that right away a headache strike me like autoclaps. But before I go lie down you see Miss Katie, I give her some licks so hot there she forget bout worm and reproduction."

"In Jesus name!"

"Yes. Is all those books her father pack her up with. Book is all him ever good for. Rather than buy food put in the pickney mouth or help Cherry find shelter his only contribution is book. Nuh his character stamp on her. No responsibility that man ever have. Look how him just take off for foreign without a word even to his lawful wife and children much less Cherry and hers. God knows where it going to end."

"Den Miss M. They really come to live with you for all time?"

"I dont know my dear. What are they to do? You know Cherry cant keep a job from one day to the next. From she was a little girl she so nervous she could never settle down long enough to anything. And you know since Papa and Mama pass away is me one she have to turn to. I tell you even if they eat me out of house and home and the child drive me to Bellevue I accept that this is the crosses that I put on this earth to bear ya Miss Katie."

"Amen. Anyway dont forget what I was saying to you about the devil. The child could have a devil inside her. No pickney suppose to come facety and force-ripe so. You better ask the Archdeacon to check it out next time he come here."

"Well. All the same Miss Katie she not all bad you know. Sometime at night when she ready to sing and dance and make up play and perform for us we laugh so till! And those times when I watch her I say to myself, this is really a gifted child."

"Well my dear is your crosses. If is so you see it then is your sister child."

"Aie. I have one hope in God and that is the child take scholarship exam and God know she so bright she bound to pass. And you know what, Miss Katie, I put her name down for the three boarding school them that furthest from here. Make them teacher deal with her. That is what they get paid for."

Beccka hiding behind the tank listening to the conversation as usual. She think about stringing a wire across the track to trip fat Katie but she feeling too lazy today. Fat Katie will get her comeuppance on Judgement Day for she wont able to run quick enough to join the heavenly hosts. Beccka there thinking of fat Katie huffing and puffing arriving at the pasture just as the company of the faithful in their white robes are rising as one body on a shaft of light. She see Katie a-clutch at the hem of the gown of one of the faithful and miraculously, slowly, slowly, Katie start to rise. But her weight really too much and with a tearing sound that spoil the solemn moment the hem tear way from the garment and Katie fall back to earth with a big buff, shouting and wailing for them to wait on her. Beccka snickering so hard at the sight she have to scoot way quick before Auntie Mary and Katie hear her. They think the crashing about in the cocoa walk is mongoose.

Beccka in Auntie Mary room – which is forbidden – dress up in Auntie Mary bead, Auntie Mary high heel shoes, Auntie Mary shawl, and Auntie Mary big floppy hat which she only wear to wedding – all forbidden. Beccka mincing and prancing prancing and mincing in front of the three-way adjustable mirror in Auntie Mary vanity she brought all the way from Cuba with her hard earned money. Beccka seeing herself as a beautiful lady on the arms of a handsome gentleman who look just like her father. They about to enter a night club neon sign flashing for Beccka know this is the second wickedest thing a woman can do. At a corner table lit by Chinese lantern soft music playing Beccka do the wickedest thing a woman can do – she take a drink. Not rum. One day Beccka went to wedding with Auntie Mary and sneak a drink of rum and stay sick for two days. Beccka thinking of all the bright-colour drink she see advertise in the magazine Cherry get from a lady she use to work for in town a nice yellow drink in a tall frosted glass...

"Beccka, Rebecca O My god!" That is Cherry rushing into the room and wailing. "You know she wi mad like hell if she see you with her things you know you not to touch her things."

Cherry grab Auntie Mary things from off Beccka and fling them back into where she hope is the right place, adjust the mirror to what she hope is the right angle, and pray just pray that Auntie Mary wont find out that Beccka was messing with her things. Again. Though Auntie Mary so absolutely neat she always know if a pin out of place. "O God Beccka," Cherry moaning.

Beccka stripped of her fancy clothes dont pay no mind to her mother fluttering about her. She take the story in her head to

71

the room next door though here the mirror much too high for Beccka to see the sweep of her gown as she does the third wickedest thing a woman can do which is dance all night.

Auntie Mary is a nervous wreck and Cherry weeping daily in excitement. The Archdeacon is coming. Auntie Mary so excited she cant sit cant stand cant do her embroidery cant eat she forgetting things the house going to the dog she dont even notice that Beccka been using her lipstick. Again. The Archdeacon coming Wednesday to the churches in the area and afterwards – as usual – Archdeacon sure to stop outside Auntie Mary gate even for one second – as usual – to get two dozen of Auntie Mary best roses and a bottle of pimento dram save from Christmas. And maybe just this one time Archdeacon will give in to Auntie Mary pleading and step inside her humble abode for tea. Just this one time.

Auntie Mary is due this honour at least once because she is head of Mothers Union and though a lot of them jealous and back-biting her because Archdeacon never stop outside their gate even once let them say anything to her face.

For Archdeacon's certain stop outside her gate Auntie Mary scrub the house from top to bottom put up back the freshly laundered Christmas Curtains and the lace tablecloth and the newly starch doilies and the antimacassars clean all the windows in the house get the thick hibiscus hedge trim so you can skate across the top wash the dog whitewash every rock in the garden and the trunk of every tree paint the gate polish the silver and bring out the crystal cake-plate and glasses she bring from Cuba twenty-five years ago and is saving for her old age. Just in case Archdeacon can stop for tea Auntie Mary bake a fruitcake a upside-down cake a three-layer cake a chocolate cake for she dont know which he prefer also some coconut cookies for although the Archdeacon is an Englishman dont say he dont like his little Jamaican dainties. Everything will be pretty and nice for the Archdeacon just like the American lady she did work for in Cuba taught her to make them.

The only thing that now bothering Auntie Mary as she give a

last look over her clean and well ordered household is Beccka, dirty Beccka right now sitting on the kitchen steps licking out the mixing bowls. The thought of Beccka in the same house with Archdeacon bring on one of Auntie Mary headache. She think of asking Cherry to take Beccka somewhere else for the afternoon when Archdeacon coming but poor Cherry work so hard and is just excited about Archdeacon coming. Auntie Mary dont have the courage to send Beccka to stay with anyone for nobody know what that child is going to come out with next and a lot of people not so broadmind as Auntie Mary. She pray that Beccka will get sick enough to have to stay in bed she – O God forgive her but is for a worthy cause – she even consider drugging the child for the afternoon. But she dont have the heart. And anyway she dont know how. So Auntie Mary take two asprin and a small glass of tonic wine and pray hard that Beccka will vanish like magic on the afternoon that Archdeacon visit.

Now Archdeacon here and Beccka and everybody in their very best clothes. Beccka thank God also on her best behaviour which can be very good so far in fact she really look like a little angel she so clean and behaving.

In fact Archdeacon is quite taken with Beccka and more and more please that this is the afternoon he decide to consent to come inside Auntie Mary parlour for one little cup of tea. Beccka behaving so well and talking so nice to the Archdeacon Auntie Mary feel her heart swell with pride and joy over everything. Beccka behaving so beautiful in fact that Auntie Mary and Cherry dont even think twice about leaving her to talk to Archdeacon in the parlour while they out in the kitchen preparing tea.

By now Beccka and the Archdeacon exchanging Bible knowledge. Beccka asking him question and he trying his best to answer but they never really tell him any of these things in theological college. First he go ask Beccka if she is a good little girl. Beccka say yes she read her Bible every day. Do you now say the Archdeacon, splendid. Beccka smile and look shy.

"Tell me my little girl, is there anything in the Bible you would like to ask me about?"

"Yes sir. Who in the Bible wrote big?"

"Who in the Bible wrote big. My dear child!"

This wasnt the kind of question Archdeacon expecting but him always telling himself how he have rapport with children so he decide to confess his ignorance.

"Tell me, who?"

"Paul!" Beccka shout.

"Paul?"

"Galations six eleven 'See with how large letters I write onto you with mine own hands'."

"Ho Ho Ho Ho" Archdeacon laugh. – "Well done. Try me with another one."

Beccka decide to ease him up this time.

"What animal saw an angel?"

"What animal saw an angel? My word. What animal ... of course. Balaam's Ass."

"Yes you got it."

Beccka jumping up and down she so excited. She decide to ask the Archdeacon a trick questions her father did teach her.

"What did Adam and Eve do when they were driven out of the garden?"

"Hm," the Archdeacon sputtered but could not think of a suitable answer.

"Raise Cain ha ha ha ha ha."

"They raised Cain Ho Ho Ho Ho Ho."

The Archdeacon promise himself to remember that one to tell the Deacon. All the same he not feeling strictly comfortable. It really dont seem dignified for an Archdeacon to be having this type of conversation with an eleven-year-old girl. But Beccka already in high gear with the next question and Archdeacon tense himself.

"Who is the shortest man in the Bible?"

Archdeacon groan.

"Peter. Because him sleep on his watch. Ha Ha Ha".

"Ho Ho Ho Ho Ho."

"What is the smallest insect in the Bible?"

"The widow's mite," Archdeacon shout.

"The wicked flee," Beccka cry.

"Ho Ho Ho Ho Ho Ho."

Archdeacon laughing so hard now he starting to cough. He cough and cough till the coughing bring him to his senses. He there looking down the passage where Auntie Mary gone and wish she would hurry come back. He sputter a few time into his handkerchief, wipe his eye, sit up straight and assume his most religious expression. Even Beccka impress.

"Now Rebecca. Hm. You are a very clever very entertaining little girl. Very. But what I had in mind were questions that are a bit more serious. Your aunt tells me you are being prepared for confirmation. Surely you must have some questions about doctrine hm, religion, that puzzle you. No serious questions?"

Beccka look at Archdeacon long and hard. "Yes," she say at long last in a small voice. Right away Archdeacon sit up straighter.

"What is it my little one?"

Beccka screwing up her face in concentration.

"Sir, what I want to know is this for I cant find it in the Bible. Please sir, do angels wear brassieres?"

Auntie Mary just that minute coming through the doorway with a full tea tray with Cherry carrying another big tray right behind her. Enough food and drink for ten Archdeacon. Auntie Mary stop braps in the dooway with fright when she hear Beccka question. She stop so sudden that Cherry bounce into her and spill a whole pitcher of cold drink all down Auntie Mary back. As the coldness hit her Auntie Mary jump and half her tray throw way on the floor milk and sugar and sandwiches a rain down on Archdeacon. Archdeacon jump up with his handkerchief and start mop himself and Auntie Mary at the same time he trying to take the tray from her. Auntie Mary at the same time trying to mop up the Archdeacon with a napkin in her mortification not even noticing how Archdeacon relieve that so much confusion come at this time. Poor soft-hearted Cherry only see that her sister whole life ruin now she dont yet

75

know the cause run and sit on the kitchen stool and throw
kitchen cloth over her head and sit there bawling and bawling in
sympathy.

Beccka win the scholarship to high school. She pass so high she
getting to go to the school of Auntie Mary choice which is the
one that is furthest away. Beccka vex because she dont want go
no boarding school with no heap of girl. Beccka dont want to go
to no school at all.
   Everyone so please with Beccka. Auntie Mary even more
please when she get letter from the headmistress setting out
Rules and Regulation. She only sorry that the list not longer for
she could think of many things she could add. She get another
letter setting out uniform and right away Auntie Mary start
sewing. Cherry take the bus to town one day with money
coming from God know where for the poor child dont have no
father to speak of and she buy shoes and socks and underwear
and hair ribbon and towels and toothbrush and a suitcase for
Beccka. Beccka normally please like puss with every new thing
vain like peacock in ribbons and clothes. Now she hardly look at
them. Beccka thinking. She dont want to go to no school. But
how to get out of it. When Beccka think done she decide to run
away and find her father who like a miracle have job now in a
circus. And as Beccka find him so she get job in the circus as a
tight-rope walker and in spangles and tights lipstick and powder
(her own) Beccka perform every night before a cheering crowd
in a blaze of light. Beccka and the circus go right round the
world. Every now and then, dress up in furs and hats like
Auntie Mary wedding hat Beccka come home to visit Cherry
and Auntie Mary. She arrive in a chauffeur-driven limousine
pile high with luggage. Beccka shower them with presents. The
whole village. For fat Katie Beccka bring a years supply of diet
pill and a exercise machine just like the one she see advertise in
the magazine the lady did give to Cherry.
   Now Beccka ready to run away. In the books, the picture
always show children running away with their things tied in a
bundle on a stick. The stick easy. Beccka take one of the walking

stick that did belong to Auntie Mary's dear departed. Out of spite she take Auntie Mary silk scarf to wrap her things in for Auntie Mary is to blame for her going to school at all. She pack in the bundle Auntie Mary lipstick Auntie Mary face powder and a pair of Auntie Mary stockings for she need these for her first appearance as a tight rope walker. She take a slice of cake, her shiny eye marble and a yellow nicol which is her best taa in case she get a chance to play in the marble championship of the world. She also take the Bible. She want to find some real hard question for the Archdeacon next time he come to Auntie Mary house for tea.

When Auntie Mary and Cherry busy sewing her school clothes Beccka take off with her bundle and cut across the road into the field. Mr O'Connor is her best friend and she know he wont mind if she walk across his pasture. Mr O'Connor is her best friend because he is the only person Beccka can hold a real conversation with. Beccka start to walk toward the mountain that hazy in the distance. She plan to climb the mountain and when she is high enough she will look for a sign that will lead her to her father. Beccka walk and walk through the pasture divided by stone wall and wooden gates which she climb. Sometime a few trees tell her where a pond is. But it is very lonely. All Beccka see is john crow and cow and cattle egret blackbird and parrotlets that scream at her from the trees. But Beccka dont notice them. Her mind busy on how Auntie Mary and Cherry going to be sad now she gone and she composing letter she will write to tell them she safe and she forgive them everything. But the sun getting too high in the sky and Beccka thirsty. She eat the cake but she dont have water. Far in the distance she see a bamboo clump and hope is round a spring with water. But when she get to the bamboo all it offer is shade. In fact the dry bamboo leaves on the ground so soft and inviting that Beccka decide to sit and rest for a while. Is sleep Beccka sleep. When she wake she see a stand above her four horse leg and when she raise up and look, stirrups, boots, and sitting atop the horse her best friend, Mr O'Connor.

"Well Beccka, taking a long walk?"

"Yes sir."

"Far from home eh?"

"Yes sir."

"Running away?"

"Yes sir."

"Hm. What are you taking with you?"

Beccka tell him what she have in the bundle. Mr O'Connor shock.

"What, no money?"

"Oooh!"

Beccka shame like anything for she never remember anything about money.

"Well you need money for running away you know. How else you going to pay for trains and planes and taxis and buy ice cream and pindar cake?"

Beccka didn't think about any of these things before she run away. But now she see that is sense Mr O'Connor talking but she dont know what to do. So the two of them just stand up there for a while. They thinking hard.

"You know Beccka if I was you I wouldnt bother with the running away today. Maybe they dont find out you gone yet. So I would go back home and wait until I save enough money to finance my journey."

Beccka love how that sound. To finance my journey. She think about that a long time. Mr O'Connor say, "Tell you what. Why dont you let me give you a ride back and you can pretend this was just a practice and you can start saving your money to run away properly next time."

Beccka look at Mr O'Connor. He looking off into the distance and she follow where he gazing and when she see the mountain she decide to leave it for another day. All the way back riding with Mr O'Connor Beccka thinking and thinking and her smile getting bigger and bigger. Beccka cant wait to get home to dream up all the tricky question she could put to a whole school full of girl. Not to mention the teachers. Beccka laughing for half the way home. Suddenly she say -

"Mr Connor, you know the Bible?"

"Well Beccka I read my Bible every day so I should think so."

"Promise you will answer a question."

"Promise."

"Mr Connor, do angels wear brassieres?"

"Well Beccka, as far as I know only the lady angels need to."

Beccka laugh cant done. Wasnt that the answer she was waiting for?

Confirmation Day

Who, if I cried, would hear me among the angelic orders?
                                        Rilke, *Duino Elegies*

IT rained the day of my confirmation. Red white and green slicks on the water which had gathered in the gutters played round my feet, winked green the gaudy tin signs of the weather-beaten shops.

EN OY APPLETON   DRINK SPRITE

My aunt had made me a dress of white gipuire which I hated and when I went into the damp mildewed vestry and they placed the veil on my head I sighed and thought of the Foolish Virgins. The mildew of the vestry and the veil and the scent of orange blossoms mingled with the smell of bats' droppings from the nave. The bats always squeaked on Sundays, competing with the squeak of the old pipe organ as Miss Miriam pedalled furiously, her white hat bobbing unbecomingly as the fury of her exultation outsped us.

My grandmother, her creamy white hair constantly fuzzing from under her hat and the feathers slithering down her face like white rats tails, always sang off-key. My aunt who they said was divorced and unhappy and who always managed to sit at the window where she could look beyond the tombstones to the curving hills beckoning never sang at all. She was small and thin-voiced and always just on the edge of our consciousness. Now she was embarrassed because my grandmother was crying as she had done on other great occasions: The Death of King George and the Coronation and my Confirmation Day.

DRINK SPRITE the signs winked green DRINK SPRITE.

In the Vestry the Beadle murmured something which I did not hear, the world was in hush: dragonflies hovered over the pond outside, butterflies waited breathlessly. I could think neither of the services nor the responses. There were six of us, all the girls in white and the boys in unaccustomed Sunday clothes and discipline wearing first-time large brown shoes that squeaked also.

The Bishop who had come to confirm us arrived in a big car, chauffeur driven. The driver did not look particularly Christian, I thought, as he leaned against the shiny new car chewing straw after straw. He had a silver-looking chain looped across his middle and from it hung a monstrously large watch which he consulted ostentatiously. He had this look of time on his face. "His watch doesn't work," whispered my cousin from behind her veil as she stood in the door beside me, "anyway I bet he can't read".

Outside, the Maguire twins whose father was the parson and who seemed the wickedest children we knew peeked from behind the vestry wall, their faces framed in flower chains. They had the same thought as my cousin for they began to sing:

One two three four
Colon man a come
With him watch chain
A lick him belly
Bam Bam Bam

Ask him for the time
And he look upon the sun

Suddenly the flowers flew into the air and they ran screaming delight behind the wall as the driver advanced toward them...

EN OY APPLETON
...in my heart I know that the world of the outside should not today concern me for says my grandmother and my aunt and the parson today I will become a child of god yet I do not know what they mean for that summer during all the catechism classes we sat at the back of the church and I listened only to the bats squeaking cows in the graveyard chomping humming-birds whirring in the guava trees outside I had only wondered why the big urn at the back was called a font and when water

was holy and the only time god ever spoke to me was on the lonely roads later as I walked home in the burning midafternoon and he raced in clouds of terror across the sky...clouds that became transformed transmuted into shapes of awe that funnelled into eternity and how could the bread and wine which my grandmother and the parson promise make me any stronger against the terrible reality of him chasing me in clouds of horror everyday...

For he always sat in the lurid church pictures of my childhood on the billowing clouds of white and his judgement was swift and terrible. He sat in the clouds on the walls of my mother's church which seemed far away and long ago...a tiny plaster church covered with pictures and showing many lands and many peoples, one repeated over and over inscribed with the words, "Light for the Lamps of Burma". I often wondered where Burma was and if it was dark there all the time unless we sent them money for lamps and I did not want to go there if they were poorer than we were...

...now we are in another time another church and the smell of incense mingles with the smell of the church and the smell is the smell of the aged. What happens to the young after their Confirmation Day? I used to wonder. Once I knew a girl who had been baptised and she had caught pneumonia and died so maybe becoming a child of God and dying were the same thing. But now the smell of starch belongs to the world of the young who never return to church after their Confirmation Day because of the terrible reality of Him. And the smell of the church is the smell of the aged and the moth balls of priests' raiments and they all belong to the other side of the world and all are in league with the clouds of terror.

And I think as the Bishop stands there in robes trimmed with gold chanting words that sound as if he speaks in a foreign language that the Confirmation will transform me too, utterly. And the smell of the church will be transformed into the smell of the bats in the nave of the church, into a world of fonts and gravestones. You get everything so mixed-up in your mind my grandmother says again and again. My mother says in no other church is there God and she is not talking of the church I am in no other my mother said one day long ago by a riverside sunlight sparkling reeds foaming round the bend...and God should have been there another day down by the same riverside when the brothers and sisters dressed in white robes who were not my brothers and sisters and the priest just a man of the people with no fussy car and driver with a watch chain to pull in and out but a man of the people took them in his arms and baptised them. But I in my white shift not gipuire but cotton my knees trembling with the early morning cold went down and fought with all my might not to go a second or third time for in the bottom of the river I had seen the mud and the reeds and the terrible reality of His existence and knew that if I went down three times I would be obliterated by His greatness. And the day became a day of the brothers and sisters who were not my brothers and sisters singing and praying praying and singing for me and my mother crying for me Oh-Oh-Ohhhhhhhhhhhhhoo-WAH mortified down by the waterside on the morning of my baptism which was not my baptism.

(Yet when she had to go not even the God of the man of the people could save her O the suffering).

This time I know that it is not easy for me to escape. The formality of my grandmother's church has woven a pattern from which it is difficult to break out, reject, just as my grandmother's life – the big house, the fixed mealtimes, the daily ritual and the necessity of Confirmation and other observances in the Book of Common Prayer created a mould into which the crazy-mad fragments of my other, disordered life were being squeezed. And so I know it is no longer a dream.

I know that I am saying the words of the Confirmation Service somewhere in my head my cousin's white dress rustles as she shifts on the velveteen cushion...and the Bishop holds a finely-wrought silver cup. He begins at the other end and I think of Oil for the Lamps of Burma which are perhaps of finely wrought silver too and the reeds in the river my mother on a sunlit day washing and my grandmother crying as she does on all great occasions and my aunt staring out the window and all the people ... and the cup is too hard against my teeth it is too large and I want to cry out and the Bishop gently forces my head back and I hardly taste the wine at all and it does not taste like the Blood of Christ. And the bread! – such a tiny little bit like eating blotting paper I squeeze my eyeballs too tight and the flames are blue and green and red and god on a cloud one day. I saw him on a cloud halfway down the road and I hid in a field behind a stone wall until the clouds finally broke into nothingness halfway across the sky.

And the congregation sings all except my aunt who remains small and sad and reminds me of saving pennies to light the Lamps of Burma and I think of lighting these lamps one by one but they remain only pinpoints of light in the darkness and I open my eyes to see if there is any light any more and the bread and wine which I have taken seem so inconsequential, so ordinary and everyday that I know I am safe. I am in a large old church with peeling plaster and damp water stains on the walls and the bats squeaking along with the squeak of the old pipe organ. And my grandmother cries as she does on all great occasions.

And standing now, facing them, I catch sight of her face in the singing congregation and she looks happy and shining. And I know it is because of me, she believes that I have been saved, become a Child of God, believes in some truth in me.

I love you grandmother but I cannot tell you. I'd rather be a child of someone else being a child of god is too frightening ...

But once outside those doors I see the Bishop's car as nothing but a small black beetle in a vast green world. I am shocked to discover a new power in myself. All that has gone before has no occasion, no meaning. I know instinctively that not the reeds in the river nor the wine nor the blood of Christ nor the Book of Common Prayer can conquer me. And not a single cloud of god is in that sky.

The Boy Who Loved Ice Cream

THEY walked down the path in single file, first the father carrying the baby Beatrice on his shoulder, then the mother, then Elsa. He brought up the rear. Wearing unaccustomed sandals, Benjy found it hard to keep his footing on the slippery path. Once or twice he almost fell and throwing out his hands to break his fall, had touched the ground. Unconsciously he wiped his hands on his seat, so that his new Sunday-go-to-church pants that his mother had made from cutting down one of his father's old jackets was already dirty with bits of mud and green bush clinging to him. But there was nobody behind him to see.

They were already late for the Harvest Festival Sale, or so his father claimed. Papa also said that it was his fault. But then his father blamed him for a lot of things, even when he was not to be blamed. The boy wasn't sure why his father was sometimes so irritable towards him, and lived in a constant state of suspense over what his father's response to him was likely to be. Now, he had been the first ready. First his sister had taken him around to the side of the house for his bath. She held him and firmly scrubbed him down with a 'strainer' covered in soap. Then she had stuck the long-handled dipper into the drum of rain water and poured it over him from head to foot. He made noises as the cold water hit him and would have run, but Elsa always had a firm grip on one of his limbs.

"Stan still yu jumbo-head bwoy or a konk yu till yu fenny," she hissed at him. Although he knew that her threats were infrequently accompanied by action beyond a slap or two, still he tried to get away from her grip for he hated this weekly ritual of bathing. But Elsa by now had learned to control him and she carried the bath through without mishap for she had whispered, "Awright. Doan have yu bath and see what happen. See if yu get no ice cream".

Ice Cream! The very words conveyed to him the sound of everything in his life that he had always wanted, always longed for, but could not give a name to. He had never tasted ice cream.

It was Elsa who had told him about it. Two years ago at the Harvest Festival Sale, Mr Doran had brought an ice cream bucket and had spent the evening the most popular man at the sale, his very customers fighting to get an opportunity to turn the bucket. According to Elsa's description, this marvellous bucket somehow produced something that, she said, was not a drink and was not food. It was hot and it was cold. Both at the same time. You didn't chew it, but if you held it on your tongue long enough it vanished, leaving an after-trace that lingered and lingered like a beautiful dream. Elsa the excitable, the imaginative, the self-assured, told him, think of your best dream, when he didn't understand. Think of it in colours, she said, pink and mauve and green. And imagine it with edges. Then imagine licking it slowly round and round the edges. That's how ice cream was.

But this description only bewildered him more. He sighed, and tried hard to imagine it. But he couldn't because he didn't have a best dream or even a good dream, only nightmares, and his mother would hold him and his father would say, "what is wrong with this pickney eh? a mampala man yu a raise". Then the baby had come and he didn't have his mother's lap any more. Now imagining ice cream, he thought of sitting cuddled in his mother's arms again and saw this mysterious new creation as something as warm and beautiful. From Elsa's description, ice cream was the most marvellous thing he had ever heard of. And the strangest. For apart from anything else, he didn't know what ice was. His thoughts kept returning to the notion of ice cream throughout the year, and soon it became the one bright constant in a world full of changeable adults.

Then last year when he would have discovered for himself

exactly what this ice cream was like, he had come down with measles. Elsa of course went to the sale for she had already had it, but he had to stay feverish and miserable with only toothless old Tata Maud to keep him company. And Elsa had come back and given him a description of ice cream that was even more marvellous than the first. This time Mr Doran had brought two buckets, and she alone had had two cones. Not even the drops, the wangla, and the slice of light cake they brought him could compensate for missing the ice cream.

This year he was well and nothing would keep him away.

Now with the thought of ice cream the cold water his sister kept splashing on him felt refreshing and he and she turned the bath into a game, both shrieking so loudly that their mother had to put her head out the window and promise to switch them both if they didn't stop.

His mother rubbed him down with an old cloth and put on his new clothes of which he was extremely proud, not noticing that the black serge was stitched very badly with white thread which was all his mother had, and the three buttons she sewed down the front were all of different sizes and colours. His shirt too, with the body of one colour, the sleeves of a print which was once part of mama's dress and the collar of yet another print, was just, Mama said, like Joseph's coat of many colours.

Then Mama had dressed the baby and she herself had got ready. By this time Papa had come up from the spring where he had had his bath and put on his Sunday suit and hat. Benjy, dressed and bored, had wandered off down to the cotton tree root to have another look at the marvellous colours and shapes of the junjo which had sprung up after the rains just a few days ago. He was so busy that it took him a long time to hear them calling. They were standing all ready to go to the Harvest Festival Sale and Papa was cross for he said that Benjy was making them late.

Papa dressed in his Sunday suit and hat was a sight to see, for he only dressed up for special occasions – funerals, weddings and the Harvest Festival Sale. Papa never went to church though Mama did every Sunday. Papa complained every Sunday that there was no hot food and dinner was always late for Mama never got back from church till late afternoon. Plus Papa never liked Mama to be away from him for any length of time.

Foolishness, foolishness, Papa said of the church going.

Mama didn't say anything but she prayed for Papa every Sunday. She wasn't that religious, but she loved every opportunity to go out. She loved to dress up and she loved to talk to people and hear all the news that was happening out there in the wide world, though she didn't believe half of it. Although Mama hadn't even been to Kingston in her life, if someone came along and said, "Let us go to the moon," quick as anything Mama would pick herself up and go. Or if Papa said to her "Let us give up all this hard life and move to town where we will have electric light and water out of a pipe and food out of a tin," Mama would not hesitate. Papa of course would never dream of saying anything of the sort. He was firmly wedded to the soil. She was always for Progress, though, as she sadly complained to the children, none of that ever came their way.

Now the Harvest Festival Sale was virtually the only time that Papa went into Springville these days. He hated to go into Springville even though it was where he was born for increasingly over the last four or five years, he had developed the feeling that Springville people knew something he didn't know but should, and they were laughing at him behind his back. It was something to do with his woman. It was one of those entirely intuitive feelings that suddenly occurred full-blown, then immediately took firm root in the mind. Even before the child was born he had had the instinctive feeling that it was not his. Then as the boy had grown, he had searched his face, his features, to discern himself there, and had failed utterly to find anything conclusive. He could never be sure. The old women used to say you could tell paternity sure thing by comparing the child's foot with that of the supposed father: "if the foot not the spitting image of the man then is jacket". He had spent countless surreptitious hours studying the turn of his son's foot but had come away with nothing. For one thing, the child was so thin and rickety that his limbs bore no resemblance to the man's heavily muscled body.

Now he had never known of the woman being unfaithful to him. But the minute she had come back from spending three weeks in Springville that time her mother was dying, from then on he had had the feeling that something had happened. Maybe it was only because she seemed to him so beautiful, so womanly that he had the first twinges of jealousy. Now every Sunday as she dressed in her neat white dress and shoes and the chaste hat which to him sat so provocatively on her head, his heart quickened as he saw her anew, not as the young girl he had taken from her mother's house so many years before, not as the gentle and good-natured mother of his children, but as a woman whom he suddenly perceived as a being attractive to other men.

But now everyone was in a good mood again as they set off down the road to the Harvest Festival Sale. First they walked a mile and a half down their mountain path where they saw no one, until they met up with the main path to the village. Always in the distance ahead of them now they could see people similarly dressed going to the sale. Others would call out to them from their houses as they passed by:

"Howdy Mis Dinah," said Papa.

"Mis Dinah," Mama said.

"Mis Dinah," the children murmured.

"Howdy Mister Seeter. Miss Mae. Children. Yu gone on early."

"Ai. Yu coming?"

"No mus'. Jus a wait for Icy finish iron mi frock Miss Mae. A ketch yu up soon."

"Awright Mis D."

Then they would walk another quarter mile or so till they got to another house perched on the hillside.

"Owdy Mister Seeter. Miss Mae. Little ones. A coming right behin."

And another family group would come out of the house and

join them. Soon, a long line of people was walking in single file down the path. The family groups got mixed. The adults would walk behind other adults so that they could talk. The children bringing up the rear instinctively ranked themselves, putting the smallest ones in front. Occasionally one of the adults would look back and frown because the tail of the line had fallen too far behind.

"Stop! Jacky! Ceddie! Mavis! Merteen! What yu all doing back there a lagga lagga so? Jus' hurry up ya pickney."

Then all the offspring chastised, the adults would soon become lost in a discussion of the tough-headedness of children.

The children paid hardly any attention and even forgot to fight or get into any mischief, for they were far too excited about the coming afternoon.

Soon, the path broadened out and joined the lane which led to the Commons where the sale was being held. Benjy loved to come out from the cool and shadows of the path, through an archway of wild brazilwood with branches that drooped so much the adults had to lift them up in order to get through. From the semi-darkness they came suddenly into the broad lane covered in marl and dazzling white which to him was the broadest street in the whole world. Today the lane was full of people as far as the eye could see, all the men in their dark suits and hats and the women, abandoning their chaste Sunday white, wearing their brightest dresses. Now a new set of greetings had to take place between the mountain people who came from a place called One Eye and were regarded as 'dark' and mysterious by the people who lived in the one-time prosperous market town of Springville. Springville itself wasn't much – a crossroads with a few wooden 'upstairs' houses with fretwork balconies, built at the turn of the century with quick money made in Panama or Cuba. Now even though these houses were so old they leaned in the wind together, and had never seen a coat of paint, to the mountain people they looked as huge and magical as anything they hoped to see. Two of these upstairs houses had shops and bars beneath, with their proud owners residing above, and on one corner there was a large one-storey concrete building with huge wooden shutters which housed the Chinese grocery and the Chinese. A tiny painted house served as the post office and the equally tiny house beside it housed Brother Brammie the tailor. The most imposing buildings in the village were the school and the Anglican Church which were both on the main lane. The Baptists and the Seventh Day Adventists had their churches on the side road.

At Harvest Festival time, all the people in the village forgot their differences and came together to support each other's Harvest Festival Sales. But none could compare in magnificence to the Anglicans'. The sale took place on the Monday after the Harvest Service in the church. On Monday morning at dawn, the church members travelled from far with the bamboo poles and coconut boughs to erect on the Commons the booths for the sale. Because the sale was a secular event and liable to attract all kinds of sinners, it was not held in the church yard but on the Commons which belonged to the church but was separated by a barbed wire fence. Since the most prosperous people in the area were Anglicans, this was the largest and most popular of the sales. After a while it became less of a traditional Harvest Festival Sale and more of a regular fair, for people began to come from the city with goods to sell, and took over a little corner of the Commons for themselves. The church people frowned on this at first, then gave up on keeping these people out even when they began to bring games such as 'Crown and Anchor', for they helped to attract larger and larger crowds which also spent money in the church members' booths. The church members also enjoyed themselves buying the wares of the town vendors, parson drawing the line only at the sale and consumption of liquor on the premises. A few zealots of the village strongly objected to this sale, forbidding their daughters to go to this den of wickedness and vice, but nobody paid these people the slightest attention. The Mothers Union ladies who had decorated the church for the Harvest Service the day before now tied up sprays of bougainvillea and asparagus fern over the entrance into each booth and radiated good cheer to everyone in their self-appointed role as hostesses.

91

The sale actually started at noon, but the only people who got there early were those who were involved in the arrangements. Most people turned up only after the men had put in at least a half-day in the fields and then gone home to bathe and dress and eat. They would stay at the sale until night had fallen, using bottle torches to light their way home.

When they got to the Commons, Benjy was the only person who was worried, for he wasn't sure that they wouldn't get there too late for the ice cream. Maybe Mr Doran would make the ice cream as soon as the sale started and then it would all be finished by the time they got there. Then another thought came: suppose this year Mr Doran was sick, or simply couldn't be bothered with ice cream any more. He would have to wait a whole year again to taste it. Perhaps never.

"Suppose, jus' suppose," he had said to his sister many times during the past week, "suppose him doan mek enough."

"Cho! As soon as him finish wan bucket him mek anadda. Ice cream nevva done," Elsa told him impatiently, wishing that she had never brought up the subject.

But this did not console him. Suppose his father refused to buy him ice cream? It was unthinkable! And yet his father's behaviour towards him was irrational: Benjy never knew just what to expect.

As soon as they turned into the Commons they could hear the sound of Mass Vass' accordion rising shrilly above the noise of the crowd, as much a part of the Harvest Festival sale as was Brother Shearer's fife and drum band that played at all fairs, weddings and other notable events for miles around.

There were so many people already in the Commons that Benjy was afraid to enter: the crowd was a living, moving thing that would swallow him up as soon as he crossed through the gate. And yet he was excited too, and his excitement won out over his fear so that he boldly stepped up to the gate where the ticket taker waited and Papa paid the entrance fee for them all.

"Now you children dont bother get lost," Mama warned them

but not too sternly, knowing that sooner or later they would all become separated in this joyous crowd.

Benjy was in an agony just to see the ice cream. But Elsa would have none of it.

"Wait nuh," she said, grabbing his hand and steering him firmly in the direction of the fancy goods stall where Mama had headed. There were cake stalls and pickles and preserves stalls, fancy goods stalls, glass cases full of baked goods and all the finest in fruits, vegetables, yams and all the other products of the soil that the people had brought to the church as their offerings to the Harvest Service. Off to one side was a small wooden merry-go-round and all over the field were children playing and shrieking.

"Elsa, ice cream," Benjy kept saying, and finally to reduce this annoyance Elsa took him over to a corner of the field where a crowd had gathered. There, she said. But the crowd was so thick that he could see nothing, and he felt a pain in his heart that so many other, bigger people also wanted ice cream. How ever would he get any?

"Nuh mine, Benjy," Elsa consoled him. "Papa wi gi wi ice cream. When de time come."

"Suppose him forget, Elsa."

"Not gwine forget."

"Yu remin' him."

"Yes."

"Promise?"

"But wa do yu ee bwoy," Elsa cried. She angrily flung his hand away and took off into the crowd.

He did not mind being alone, for this rich crowd so flowed that sooner or later the same people passed each other.

Benjy wished he had some money. Then he would go and wiggle his way into the very centre of the crowd that surrounded the ice cream bucket. And he would be standing there just as Mr Doran took out the ice cream. But he didn't know anything about money and had no idea what something as wonderful as ice cream would cost.

So he flowed with the crowd, stopping here and there but not really looking at anything and soon he came across his mother with Beatrice. Mama firmly took hold of his hand.

"Come. Sister Nelson bring a piece of pone fe yu."

She took him to Sister Nelson who gave him the pone which he stuffed into his mouth.

"Say tank yu chile. Yu doan have manners?" his mother asked.

He murmured thank you through the pone. Sister Nelson smiled at him. "Growing a good boy," she said and patted his head.

"But baad!" Mama said, laughing.

Mama was always saying that and it frightened him a little, for he never knew for sure just how he was 'baad'.

"Mama," he said, "ice cream".

"Chile! Yu mout full an yu talking bout ice cream aready!"

Tears started to trickle down his cheeks.

"Now see here. A bawl yu wan' bawl? Doan mek a give yu something fe bawl bout, yu hear bwoy. Hm. Anyway a doan know if there is money for foolishness like cream. Have to see yu father about dat."

His heart sank, for the day before he had heard his father complain that there was not enough money to buy all the things they needed at the Harvest Festival Sale and did she think money grew on trees. But everyone knew that Papa saved all year for that day, for the town vendors came and spread out their wares under the big cotton tree – cloth, pots and pans, fancy lamps, wicks and shades, readymade clothes, shoes, shoe-laces, matches, knives, cheap perfume, plastic oilcloths for the table, glasses with birds and flowers, water jugs, needles, en-amelware, and plaster wall hangings with robins and favourite bible texts. Even Miss Sybil who had the dry goods store would turn up and buy from them, and months later the goods would turn up in her dark and dusty shop at twice the price as the vendors'.

Mama had announced months in advance that she wanted an oilskin cloth, a new lampshade and shoes for the children. She hadn't mentioned anything for herself, but on these occasions Mama usually came home with a pair of new shoes, or a scarf, or a hat – anything that would put her in touch with what seemed another, glamorous life.

Papa, like his son, was distracted, torn between two desires. One was to enjoy the sale and to see if he could pick up anything for the farm or just talk to the farmers whom now-adays he never saw at any other time. Then the Extension Officer was there and he wanted to catch him to ask about some new thing he had heard that the government was lending money to plant crops though he didn't believe a word of it. Then he wanted to go and buy a good white shirt from the town vendors. Mama had insisted that he should. And he wanted to see the new games they had brought. In many ways one part of his mind was like a child's, for he wanted to see and do everything. But another part of his mind was spoiling the day for him: he didn't want to let Mama out of his sight. More and more the conviction had been growing on him that if there had been another man in her life, it wasn't anyone from around here. So it had to be a townman. And where else did one get the opportunity to meet strangers but at the sale. Walking down the mountain path he had started out enjoying the feeling of going on an outing, the only one he permitted himself for the year. But as they got nearer and nearer to Springville and were joined by other people, he became more and more uneasy. The way his woman easily greeted and chatted with people at first used to fill him with pride and admiration that she could so naturally be at ease where he was dull and awkward and clumsy. But by the time they entered the lane this pride had turned to irritation, for now he had begun to exaggerate in his mind precisely those qualities for which he had previously praised her: now she laughed too loudly, chattered too much, she was not modest enough, she attracted attention to herself – and to him, for having a woman so common and so visible. By the time they got to the Commons it was clear to her that he was in one of his 'moods' though she did not know why and she hoped that the crowd would bring back his good humour again, for she was accustomed to his ups and downs. But she didn't dwell on the man's moods, for nothing would make her not enjoy herself at the sale.

Now the man surreptitiously tried to keep her under his eye but it was virtually impossible because of the crowd. He saw her sometimes only as a flash in the distance and he strained to see what she was up to, but he caught her only in the most innocent of poses – with church sisters and married couples and little children. She eagerly tried on hats and shoes. She looked at pictures. She examined tablecloths. She ate grater cake and snowballs. Looking at her from afar, her gestures seemed to him to pure, so innocent that he told himself that he was surely mad to think badly of her. Then he looked at the town folk gathered around the games, hawking yards of cloth, and stockings and ties and cheap jewellery. He looked at them and their slim hard bodies and their stylish clothes and their arrogant manners and their tough faces which hid a knowledge of the world he could never have. And he felt anxious and angry again. Now he turned all his attention to these townmen to see if he could single out one of them: the one. So engaged did he become on this lonely and futile pursuit that he hardly heard at all what anybody said to him. Even the children begging for ice cream he roughly brushed aside. He was immediately full of remorse, for he had planned to treat them to ice cream, but by the time he came to his senses and called after them, they had disappeared into the crowd. He vowed that once he met up with them again he would make up for his gruffness. He would treat them not only to ice cream but to sliced cake, to soft drinks, to paradise plums and jujubs. But the moment of softness, of sentiment, quickly passed for his attention became focussed on one man in black pants and a purple shirt and wearing a grey felt hat. The man was tall, brown-skinned and good looking with dark, curly hair. He couldn't tell why this man caught his attention except that he was by far the best looking of the townmen, seemed in fact a cut above them, even though like some of the others his arms were covered from wrist to elbow in lengths of cheap chains, and his fingers in the tacky rings that he was selling. He watched the man steadily while he flirted and chatted with the girls and finally faded out of sight – but not in the direction his woman was last seen.

Now Benjy was crying and even Elsa felt let down. Papa had refused to buy them ice cream! Although she cajoled and threatened, she couldn't get Benjy to stop crying. He was crying as much for the ice cream as for being lost from even his mother so happy and animated among all the people she knew, amid crowds and noise and confusion. Now she had little time for them and impatiently waved them on to 'enjoy themselves'. Elsa did just that for she found everything entertaining and school friends to chatter with. But not Benjy. She could not understand how a little boy could be so lacking in joy for such long periods of time, and how his mind could become focussed on just one thing. If Benjy could not have ice cream, he wanted nothing.

Night was coming on and they were lighting the lamps. They hung up the storm lantern at the gate but all the coconut booths were lit with kitchen bitches. Only the cake stall run by Parson's wife and the most prosperous ladies of the church had a tilly lamp, though there wasn't much cake left to sell.

Benjy still stumbled along blindly, dragged by Elsa who was determined to get a last fill of everything. Benjy was no longer crying but his eyes were swollen and he was tired and his feet were dragging. He knew that soon they would have to go home. The lighting of the lamps was the signal for gathering up families together, and though they might linger for a while after that talking, making last minute purchases and plans, children were at this point not allowed to wander or stray from the group for the word of adults had once again become law, and when all the adults decided to move, woe onto the child who could not be found.

So everyone was rounding up everyone else, and in this confusion, Benjy started to howl again for he and Elsa were passing by Mr Doran and his bucket, only the crowd was so thick around it you couldn't see anything.

But just then they ran into Papa again and, miraculously, he was the one that suggested ice cream. Although Benjy's spirits immediately lifted, he still felt anxious that Papa would never be able to get through that crowd in time. Papa left him and Elsa on the fringes, and he impatiently watched as Papa, a big man, bore his way through. What is taking Papa so long? I bet Mr Doran has come to the end of the bucket. There is no more ice cream. Here comes Mr Manuel and Mars Edgy asking if they aren't ready. And indeed, everyone from the mountain was more or less assembled and they and Papa now seemed the only people missing from the group. They told Mars Edgy that Papa had gone to get them ice cream, and Mars Edgy was vexed because, he said, Papa should have done that long before. Now Mars Edgy made his way through the crowd around the ice cream vendor and Benjy's hopes fell again. He felt sure that Mars Edgy would pull Papa away before he got the ice cream. Torn between hope and despair, Benjy looked up at the sky which was pink and mauve from the setting sun. Just like ice cream! But here comes Papa and Mars Edgy now and Papa is carrying in his hands three cones and Papa is coming and Benjy is so excited that he starts to run towards him and he stumbles and falls and Elsa is laughing as she picks him up and he is laughing and Mars Edgy is moving off quickly to where the mountain people are standing and Papa bends down and hands him a cone and Papa has a cone and Elsa has a cone and Benjy has a cone and the three of them stand there as if frozen in time and he is totally joyous for he is about to have his first taste of ice cream but even though this is so long-awaited so precious he first has to hold the cone at arm's length to examine it and witness the ice cream perched just so on top and he is afraid to put it into his mouth for Elsa said it was colder than spring water early in the morning and suppose just suppose it burns his tongue suppose he doesn't like it and Elsa who is well into eating hers and Papa who is eating his are laughing at him... then he doesn't know what is happening for suddenly Papa sees something his face quickly changes and he flings away his cone and makes a grab for Benjy and starts walking almost running in the direction where Mama is standing she is apart from all the people talking to a strange man in a purple shirt and Papa is moving so fast Benjy's feet are almost off the ground and Benjy is crying Papa Papa and everything is happening so quickly he doesn't know the point at which he loses the ice cream and half the cone and all that is left in his hand is the little tip of the cone which he clutches tightly and he cannot understand why Papa has let go of his hand and is shouting and why Mama isn't laughing with the man anymore and why everyone is rushing about and why he has only this little tip of cone in his hand and there is no ice cream and he cannot understand why the sky which a minute ago was pink and mauve just like the ice cream is now swimming in his vision like one swollen blanket of rain.

Ballad

TEACHER ask me to write composition about The Most Unforgettable Character I Ever Meet and I write three page about Miss Rilla and Teacher tear it up and say that Miss Rilla not fit person to write composition about and right away I feel bad the same way I feel the day Miss Rilla go and die on me.

When Miss Rilla die I wish I could make up a Ballad for her like they do for famous people in the old days. Dont ask me why only when we sing ballad song in school I get sad and think of Miss Rilla. But I cant sing or play guitar and nobody make music round here since that Blue Boy gone away and beside this whole thing too deep and wide for a little thing like a Ballad. So I will just tell you the story of Miss Rilla and Poppa D, Blue Boy and me though is really about Miss Rilla. And when we come to the sad part we can have something like a chorus because they have that in all the ballad song they sing but I dont think bout the chorus yet.

Miss Rilla die on truck that was carrying her to market and they bring her body back down but I never see it before they make it one with the Springville ground for all day I down by the river crying and not crying, laughing and not laughing.

O my Lord. Miss Rilla dont laugh round here anymore and it seem like all the laughing in the world come to a stop and everybody talking nice bout her. Eh-eh everybody talking like they never once say any nastiness and like Blue Boy would say if he was here, "It grieve me so Lord". Is same way Blue Boy would say only he dont talk much because all the time he there playing music on one fife he did make himself and this music tall and pale and thin just like him and not like anything you ever hear over Mass Curly radio.

To show you how Blue Boy never talk much: the night Joe
Amos come from town with news that Miss Rilla drop dead on
truck every jack man in Springville have something to say.
Except Blue Boy. He never say anything at all. Blue Boy just
stick him fife in him pocket and he leave only I dont know is
gone he gone forever till him mother come from over Laplands
the Sunday and say nobody see him anywhere and where he is.
And when I say I dont know she give me bad eye for me and
Blue Boy always keeping company but it wasnt what anybody
think at all so I dont pay her no mind. Any nobody see him to
this day although I have strong feeling he gone Kingston to get
·on Talent Show on radio and if he evèr come back to this place
at all he will change change.

So now Blue Boy sort of walk through my mind but not Miss
Rilla. Blue Boy pass through my mind because I dont remember
music in my mind. But every now and then when something
really sweet me I will break into a loud loud laugh and sometimes when I listen back to this laugh is just like Miss Rilla
herself laughing.

Even MeMa notice it for the other day she say to me,
"Lenora, cut out that nasty piece of laughing for you beginning
to sound just like Rilla Dunvil" only by the time she say it I not
laughing any more I crying but not so she can see.

MeMa never cry for Miss Rilla. MeMa never cry for nobody.
And she did have some harsh word to say about Miss Rilla and
Blue Boy – the only people in the world that I love.

Bwoy, hear what she say bout Blue Boy when she see him
passing on roadside:

"Look at that wutless good-fe-nutten a gwan there nuh.
Whoever hear bout a big man a-play on a half-ass piece of
bamboo all day long, tell me nuh? But what you expect no
Laplands he come from? An' let me tell you that nutten good
ever come out of that backward place and that is the Lord own
truth. Is pure Coromantee nigger live over there like that bwoy
Zackie that did tief Mass Curly goat yu no see how the lot of
them redibo and have puss eye? Just like that musicman friend
of yours there. He might be yu cousin out of wedlock that yu

father brother Rennis did have on the side with that Coromantee woman and blood thicker than water but I still dont see why you have to mix yuself up with that trash because everybody trying hard to bring yu up in a good Christian home with decent people children. Anyway bird of a feather flock together and everybody know your pedigree not so hot so if is that class of people yu want to mix up wid dog nyam yu supper. Yu can gwan yu is yu father pickney and he will have to deal with yu I not going worry myself no more."

When MeMa go on so I just sit quiet quiet till she forget what she talking bout because if I make any sound she quick to fire me a box hot-hot. I call her MeMa though she really not my mother at all. She is the mother of Elsie and George and Rainey and Marshall and Petey and Dulcie and Gabriel but their pa Mass George is my Pa too only he did have me with a lady friend he was keeping one time over at Morningside. But she did have other children from before I born and MeMa did take me from I small and raise me up in her house because she say she couldnt stand the embarrassment that it cause with her church sister and all to see me as a Barstard round the place. And generally she not so bad though she say some word that really hurt sometime and I know that she dont love me like her own children but that Miss Rilla love me because she dont have no other children to love.

So whenever MeMa done quarrel and gone round the back I wait till her attention distracted and I run down to Miss Rilla yard where I know Blue Boy waiting under the jacaranda tree and Miss Rilla sitting in her rocking chair eating her own sweet things she bake in the oven that Poppa D make for her round the back and I so happy my two people in the world waiting for me.

O God but sometime MeMa go on bad about people so, especially about Miss Rilla. Miss Rilla will walk past in her pretty red dress and her new head tie and some big gold earring hanging down and Poppa D new boots and I think she looking like a million pound and like Missis Queen herself.

"Aie there Miss Grett, w'appen," she call out smiling and

waving her hankie at MeMa who there hanging out clothes on the line.

"Holdin steady me darling, holdin steady me chile," MeMa call out in her sweet-sweet voice and the clothes pin she holding drop from her mouth. "Stop! Is how yu looking so blooming today me dear?"

"Aie, a not feeling so well all the same yu know but I cant complain," Miss Rilla say and she fanning and wiping her face for the day really hot.

I a-listen from round the side of the house and I know them two set of eye make one and then the two of them look way quick-quick and is only silence I hear.

Then Miss Rilla say slow-like, "Well, a jus a run a Mass Curly shop to get a little oil before dark for Poppa D never remember bring me a drop from town."

"Eh-eh, then no so life stay me dear. Anyway some of we not even so lucky to have people bring we things from town ha-ha," MeMa say. "But walk good me dear."

All this time she talking in her sweet-sweet voice and she watch Miss Rilla walk slow-like up the road because Miss Rilla carry plenty weight on her body and the rockstone them really hard.

As soon as Miss Rilla outa earshot and MeMa take her in she run inside quick time and bawl out for my big sister Dulcie and Estrella that does wash for us sometime. "Ai Dulcie, Estrella, come look at this pappyshow no mi chile." And the whole lot of them run outside to crane them neck up the road.

"Eh-eh, Mother-young-gal brucking style today papa," say the Dulcie she.

"She really looking blooming me dear I tell her though I would look blooming to if I was brazen enough so put all that rouge thing on my face," MeMa say.

"An her earring look just like cartwheel. Is who she trying fool say is gold?"

"An is poor Poppa D good boot she a-wear out," Estrella say as if is her boot. "Lord, Jackass say worl no level an is true because look how that man work him finger to the bone an all the woman do is wear out him good boot on the rockstone jus because she wan bus style."

And then they say plenty more thing and they go on like that every time Miss Rilla even step out of her yard.

O Lord. No more laughing. No more big gold earring. No more Miss Rilla gizada to cool down me temper when MeMa beat me. All the sweetness done.

II

"Hi yu little crying chile with the red head. Come here," Miss Rilla call out the day I pass her house just after she move down from Red Ground. "Come here, you is a Gayle without a doubt. What yu crying for?"

O Lord Miss Rilla larger than my whole life sitting on a rocking chair Poppa D make for her but it splintering now and I learn when she ask question she dont want answer for she using her apron to wipe my eye and when she done I get a good look at her. I did think Miss Rilla was a gypsy woman though I never in my life see no gypsy but that is how she look. To Gawd! And me eye water done quick quick for she gone inside the house and I studying how a big woman can move so light and she come back out with a plateful of gizada that big and juicy and hot, and quick, I forget bout beating and eye water.

"Little sweetness always cure bad temper. Never mind though chile yu forget the hurt by the time yu marry. But take care yu dont marry already for when eveningtime come I see you with that boy that play the music so sweet the two of you nice-up past here eveningtime yu think I dont see you."

By this time Miss Rilla laughing and laughing the way she laugh when she teasing people and she didnt have in her false teeth the first time I see her and her mouth wide open in a O in her big big laugh.

Before Miss Rilla laughing I never hear woman really laugh before, think only man know how to give deep belly laugh.

Miss Rilla used to bake things and keep in a glass case and

sell them to schoolchildren and big people that pass. But most of the time she take her sweet things to Kingston to sell on sidewalk. She would travel up to Kingston with the rest of the higgler on Mass Curly truck that Poppa D use to drive. People did say that is not that she really need the money but that she dont trust Poppa D out of her sight and some people say that is the other way round but I dont business with that.

Anyway is same truck that Miss Rilla die on. Her heart just give way 'cording to Big Mout Doris. Is Big Mout Doris did tell the whole story to MeMa and MeMa just interrupting interrupting all the time and is bout Miss Rilla I want to hear.

"We jus have to wait in the middle of the sunhot you know Miss Grett, yes mam," Big Mout Doris say. "Cephas had was to get ride to May Pen to get Strongman and Strongman get ride to where we all was and drive we to town. Poppa D did want the truck was to turn back and go straight home but by this time all we food spoiling in the sunhot and is not the people hard you understand but is we livelihood that and pickney still a yard fe keep alive so we had was to reach town.

"So when Poppa D introduce this argument tho we all grieve we couldnt do nutten bout it. Him there a cry and a say how police a town going take him wife body weh and not give him back and how him did promise bury her under jacaranda tree in garden so when she dead she can still hear tree branch a su-su. Some people extra yu know maam...

"To tell yu truth we nevva like the dead body on the truck but she didnt look so bad you know she just look like seh she sleeping and how we did fine out that is dead she dead is that she did lean over on Jennie on the bench and Jennie say 'Hi Miss Rilla allow me to breathe no man you heavy to support yu know and we all want catch we little sleep before we reach town'.

"Then Jennie did try ease her back on her side of the bench and all the try she try she couldnt budge her for she like dead weight and then Jennie touch her and notice that she cold cold so she try wake her and she callin and shoutin so hard she wake up everybody else in the truck but not Miss Rilla and then

Jennie give out 'Lord Jesus I think is dead Miss Rilla dead on me' and everybody start bawl out fe Jesus and we finally come to a real understanding that is dead she dead in truth so we knock on the window to get Poppa D to stop the truck and at last he must study that something wrong for he stop the truck and he come round the back and he shout out: 'Is what happen to the whole lot of you eh?'

"An we didnt have the heart to tell him that Miss Rilla dead so we say: 'We dont think Miss Rilla feelin so well Poppa D' and he say 'eh-eh' and climb in the truck and start feel her hand and her face and then he feel her heart and he saying 'Miss Rill Miss Rill' quiet-like and when he feel her heart he find out that it not beating at all so now he turn round and look at all of we standing outside round the back of the truck a look up at him and we all quiet and when he look at we all he did say was 'Why you all didnt tell me she dead eh' and none of we did know what to say to that.

"So he just sit there a hold her hand and everything quiet like it quiet onto death and we never even notice that day breaking round we and everybody coughing and slapping the mosquito them and not saying nothing and we shifting we foot because we dont know what to do till finally Cephas clear him throat and Cephas say, 'Poppa D we know is hard and we is all grieving with you but we cant stay here all day and sunhot coming up'.

"This was to get Poppa D to do something but he never say nothin and by this time we all by the roadside and a start argue so finally – you know how Cephas have a word for every occasion – finally Cephas say 'Listen now Poppa D is in no fit state to drive we and since none of we can drive this truck we have to find somebody else to drive. Is not that I cant drive you know I can drive good good but like how that tiefing bwoy up May Pen fail me when I go take Test because I never give him more than four shilling the ol dawg I dont want get in no trouble with police'.

"So we there arguing again and by this time Poppa D crying and say how we have to go back to Springville and we say we cant do that for our livelihood on that truck so Cephas go get Strongman and Strongman come back and drive me. And we telling Poppa D he better off siddown in front with Strongman because he would have to direct him when he reach town seeing as how Strongman dont know town so good. So we manage to get him to the truck front because all the time he like a man in a dream and Miss Rilla look like she still asleep though nobody sitting beside her now. And Cephas say 'Look here this is a time of sadness and the Bible say that we must respect the dead, amen. But I think we doing the right thing and God will smile on we because he understand we is all poor people and we must look after we living and if we dont sell we things we living dont eat. But I dont think that we should tell anybody in town there is a dead on this truck with this food for them Kingston people is very foolish and suspicious and they would never buy food from Springville people again. So we better take the food off quick as we reach and leave Miss Rilla with Poppa D and Strongman to look after'.

"So Strongman tell we afterward that Poppa D still confuse up when we reach and he didnt know what to do but Strongman see a Special that he did know from long time – is Jane Southwell from Red Groun pickney that she did have with the Adams bwoy from Montego Bay and him turn out good-good and get job with Police – so Strongman call him one side and tell him that we have a dead body on the truck and the Special dont believe but he look inside and he see the body in truth so him study for a while and then him say as cording to how things stay Strongman better take the body to morgue for if police find out is plenty trouble. So after one piece of argument with Poppa D that is what they do.

"Anyway I hear that they still have plenty confusion with police and Poppa D did have to pay plenty money to have the body embalm and they bring it back down in a special big black car pretty cant done. I didnt see it but Jennie tell me that them embalmer man in Kingston did fix her up real nice and she did have a lovely funeral but I couldnt go because the youngest Eda sick bad again and coughing the whole night...I tell you one thing though Miss Grett, that Poppa D not himself at all from it happen. I never see a man take death so hard in all me born days and when you consider what she is... Anyway, they say you mustnt say bad bout the dead and I dont have a thing personal against her you understand because plenty time she really kind to the pickney them. But since the funeral Poppa D just sit on the same rocking chair she herself use to siddown on and is like him dont see nothing that a go on in front of him eye. Is like he looking down inside himself all the time. But maam, if I was him I wouldnt look down inside my soul at all for I would fraid what I see. They say what is past is past and is water under bridge nuh, but the Lord say that retribution for your sin will catch up with you. Is not everybody die on truck that going to town Miss Grett, is not a Christian death that at all at all .. While I never say nutten bad about the dead and nothing personal bout Miss Rilla none of the two of them can really expect to have a good death after all they have on their conscience and I would not surprise if she not resting easy herself. In fact I hope they planning a good burydown with plenty rum and praying for if her duppy come back is sure to turn rolling calf because she did even look like coolie sometime and everybody know how coolie duppy bad.

"Anyway I cant linger with you at all today for the baby still have the grippe bad but I hear say Mass Curly having a hard time getting somebody to drive that truck and if another truck did pass by I would prefer to take it. Poppa D burn out just good fe nutten me dear maam... Anyway I sorry I cant stay for a good labrish but is gone me gone now and as they say cockroach no business inna fowl roost but is really a hard thing that happen to Poppy D".

Ai, no more laughing. No more Miss Rilla come back from market bringing me a pocket comb or a hair ribbon. Only Poppa D and I hurry pass the house and dont say a word. It dont matter. Poppa D dont see nobody dont see me.

III

Now it look like I gone and spoil this ballad story for this is not the way I want to tell it at all. The part about Miss Rilla dying is the end part and it really should start at the beginning. Only to tell you the truth I dont know the beginning or end of anything right now for I still grieve over my lovely friend Miss Rilla that gone and die on me. And I suppose to sit exam this year for scholarship to high school but Teacher go and tell MeMa I not learning at all and he say is a sin because I am a bright girl especially at the english language he say and could become teacher or nurse or something like that. So MeMa beat me for I not learning and she say she dont understand how I turn worthless in school nowadays considering that my two distraction Miss Rilla and Blue Boy not here anymore to turn me fool.

To tell you truth I dont think MeMa mind if I dont pass exam because I dont think she like how I come bright in school and Teacher always praising me and none of her own children so bright. And I think she vex because I am me father outside child and I come bright. And although she listen to Teacher and beat me when I dont study hard and tell Teacher she want to do her best for me even though I not her child, at the yard she say when she vex:

"Dont bother get no idea into your head bout pass exam and go high school and that sort of impertinence for none of my rightful children them reach high school yet and I dont know what make you think you better than them and I know is that teacher there putting idea into your head that you so bright that make you carrying on this extraness. But teacher only like you because you darker than my children and is only that you red and not so black like him and everybody saying how black man time come now and they all sticking together and my children come out too good colour to suit him. Thats why he never encouragement them and make them fail they exam all the time because they come out with good colour and straight hair better than Chiney hair and everybody know this country going to the dog these days for is pure black people children they pushing to send high school. Anybody ever hear you can educate monkey? Well in that case I dont care if my children dont go because nobody of consequence going to them old high school anymore. Anyway that teacher man forming fool though. Dont bother make him put no more idea into your head for I take you from you was a baby and raise you up in good Christian home and spend money clothe and feed you and give you book and slate and pencil for school just like I give my own children and I never once treat you different from them in any way at all and I do this from the bottom of my heart because the Bible say 'Suffer little children to come onto me' so dont bother make teacher turn you fool . . ."

Is so she go on and she slap the iron on the coal pot and grab a new one and when she wipe it done on the banana trash she slamming it down on the clothes the same way. Some time for so long she wouldnt say a word that I try walk way slow-like but she would see me and start up again.

"Where you think you going when I talking to you yu unmannersable little wretch you? Wait! You think say is yu friend them you with?"

And then she slam down the iron again and make up her face over the ironing and every move she make jerky and fast like she vex. Not like Miss Rilla who do everything slow-like, the same way she walk. But as MeMa talking she slamming down the iron like comma.

"I cant afford to send my own children to high school so I dont know who you think have money to send you and you should be thinking now that your place is here in this yard to care for your father and me in our old age because my rightful children not staying round here forever. No sir. They all going to town to get good job in store because their coloration is good and everybody know that them big office and store in Kingston dont want no natty head pickney work with them. So my advice to you is learn some sewing and things like that so you can stay right here and take care of we and help pay for you keep and is a pity your head so natty and red for your coloration not so bad but you wont find no nice man married to you for they dont want no natty head pickney. They looking for wife with good coloration so they can raise the colour so just learn sewing and forget the books them."

But MeMa wasnt so bad even when she say words that really hot me is like she not talking to me at all is like she talking to the clothes she ironing or the pot she stirring or whatever she doing at the time. And even though she not me own ma she did take me in from I small and raise me up and I am grateful only she make me feel very small sometime when she start talking bout me and now between she and Teacher she really have me confuse because Teacher and Teacher Wife say:

"Lenora you are a good girl and if you only put your head to the books you can get a scholarship and go to high school and even teacher college and be a credit to all of us but this last year you havent even tried... Lenora dont you want to be a teacher dont you want to be a nurse...?"

And I confuse confuse because one mind in me say that I should study and pass exam so that I can go to high school and speak good and wear pretty dress and high heel shoes like Miss Martin the other teacher and Teacher Wife who is also a teacher and I think it would really grieve Dulcie to see me succeed like that because she always fas'ing with me head and I have to wear her old dress and she tell everybody is ol bruck I wear but is only because she stupid and cant pass anything at all and even though she older than me Teacher put us in the same class and if I turn Teacher I could get me hair straighten just like Teacher Wife. And I confuse because another voice say that MeMa will vex and she wont give me any encouragement even if I pass scholarship and Pa say he dont business. And she might send me back to my mother who I dont even know and who I hear have more children since she have me and she never once send me a Paradise Plum or come to see how I grow. So maybe I should learn sewing or how to be postmistress and stay round here so I can take care of Pa and MeMa in their old age

111

because even if I go high school and study all the people at the bank still have fair skin with good hair and suppose I dont want teach I dont know if I could get work anywhere else.

O Lord I confuse confuse. No Miss Rilla to tell me what to do. No Blue Boy playing music. No nobody to tell me nothing.

IV

Like the time when I was little and I ask MeMa where baby come from and MeMa lick me on me head same time with the coconut brush she cleaning floor with and me on my knees beside her polishing and she lick me such a blow I drop and she say:

"But what in Jesus name is the matter with this pickney eh? Is force-ripe woman this? What you want to fass in big people business for? Baby is big people business chile so dont form fool of yourself and ask impertinent question. Is who put idea into your head eh? Well Jehosiphat! I never see or hear such a thing. I have big daughter and them never have the face so come and ask me bout them things so you just wait your turn pickney for if you so force-ripe to be asking them things at your age next thing I know you go try out what you learn and braps we have another bastard in this house."

But I did know a girl who wasnt much older than me and she did start to make baby even though it die and a girl at school tell me things that I dont believe and I dont know why MeMa so confuse when I ask her a little thing like that. So I decide to go ask Miss Rilla but I dont know if she know anything because she dont have no children and Poppa D dont have none neither and I dont know if you have to have children first before you know anything bout them.

So I ask Miss Rilla because I know she wont vex and lick me but bredda! She there in her rocking chair shelling peas and I helping her and her eyes look far far away like she considering and she consider a long time till her hands stop shell the peas and she sort of give a little sigh and she say:

"Well Lenora child I cant tell you in nice word because I dont know none but I not sure that you not too young to know bout them things but since you ask is man put seed in the woman belly and it ripen and nine month afterward you conceive and have baby.

"But listen child this is all I going to tell you because I dont want give you any idea bout baby now, you is to go and do your studies and train and turn teacher and when you grow up big you will meet a nice teacher man or a agriculture man with good government job and you will marry and he can do it to you so you can make baby. But dont worry about them things finish you education and dont bother interest yourself in man at all they is pure trouble..."

She continue to shell peas and when she didnt laugh her eyes big and shiny like ackee seed only them sad sad like picture I see all the time of Mary Jesus Mother. Her face strong, stronger than any face I ever see and we shell peas till it quiet like death.

"Miss Rilla then how come you and Poppa D living together all this while and you dont have children?"

More silence and I watch her hand stop.

"Ai child, some things you just cant explain... God decide that some people not to have children because there is too much suffering children in the world already and they dont have enough food to feed them but is not you decide though is God decide and you just have to accept what he say ...

I want to ask her more but I fraid for Miss Rilla looking sad on me and I never see her look so sad before.

But I hear them talking, I hear the women talking when they over at MeMa house or down by river washing, talking say she is mule because she barren and that God ordain all women to have children and if woman dont have children she no better than mule because God curse is on her and then they talk about the wicked thing that Miss Rilla do and how she is harlot.

So when Miss Rilla tell me why she dont have children I still confuse but I believe is God say that she not to have children for too many sad children in world already and I know my rightful mother did have a whole heap of children before she have me

113

and she didnt have enough food to feed them so she give them away and maybe God say that she should have me so that I can be a blessing to MeMa and Pa in their old age but I dont know.

But I know this wicked thing they talking about that Miss Rilla do, I listen bout the yard and I been hearing it from I was a child. Not until about two years ago when I really old that I get to know Miss Rilla for she living in another district all this time with Poppa D until Poppa D decide to build the house near we so we turn neighbours. But this thing that happen did happen long before I ever born and I hear so much about it that even now I dont believe that it happen around here and is like the Miss Rilla they all talking about is another Miss Rilla and is not the lady I really know because I never see Miss Rilla do anything bad and everybody say that the other Miss Rilla do a wicked wicked thing and the Bible say anybody who do a thing like that will perish in everlasting hell fire. So they say.

But even though she dead I cant believe Miss Rilla in any hell fire. I know she is in Heaven though MeMa say she is the main sinner in Jamaica and look how she dont even go to church. But if you ask me Miss Rilla fly straight up to Heaven and she up there with Saint Peter and living in a little house with a rocking chair on the verandah just like her house on earth because it was so pretty and she did love it so. And she still making gizada and grater cake, wangla and drops, and all the little children in Heaven round her and she teasing them and telling them stories and they laughing all the time. Up there even the big people are her friends because nobody talk nasty about nobody in Heaven. So Miss Rilla just keeping everybody up in Heaven laughing and because she look so pretty and like Missis Queen when she dress up they ask her to wear her red dress to brighten up Heaven even though everybody suppose to wear white. And when Saint Peter see Miss Rilla in her red dress and her glass case full of bake things he say this is just what Heaven need and he get the mason up there to build her a brick oven just like the one Poppa D did make for her and she there baking gizada and grater cake, wangla and drops and all sort of sweet thing in Heaven.

So I dont see why they did have to go on bout keep up no big Nine Night for her when she die and everybody drinking up the rum and them all talking bout planting her down real deep or else her duppy come back like rolling calf which is bad duppy to haunt you. Cho! Miss Rilla have better things to do with her time in heaven than think about this District where all they do is backbite her and they not even worth haunting anyhow.

This is how I think sometime but to tell you the truth I not sure because I feel kind of jealous now that Miss Rilla have a whole lot of other children to joke with and sometime I want to die too so that I can be with her. And sometime I not so sure that she really gone to Heaven at all since from the time I know her she never even go to church. I only know no more bake things, no more Miss Rilla, all the laughing done.

V

Is the same way she disappear the day after the murder and nobody can find her, nobody at all, and everybody looking all over the place. And the police all round a-take statement and a-measure and a-write things down in book and they couldnt find her neither and they did want to ask her all sort of question and everybody round the place a excite up themself because nothing like this ever happen before and everybody saying that it give the district a bad name and even people in Kingston get to hear bout it for it Gleaner, and they say round here that from she born she causing trouble.

And everybody arguing say what they would do if it was them and some people saying that they cant blame her if she run away for they would shame and run way too if it was them and some people say that the best thing that she could ever do is hang herself or drop into sinkhole. And they say that if she ever show herself in the district again they would stone her to death because that is what they do in the Bible to people like that. And MeMa say that no matter where Miss Rilla flee whether to hills or valleys Gods justice will find her and punish her because

God is a just God and he is everywhere and he find all sinners and punish them no matter where they hide even if they quick or dead, fast or slow. And they search and search and no Miss Rilla until the excitement almost die down. Pa say that after a time Springville people never care if they find Miss Rilla because people use to drive down there in motor car to see the place where all the excitement was happening and such a thing never happen before and they never see so much motor car in their life and all the boy them half the time so busy looking at motor car they forget about Miss Rilla. And that Agnes Dawson who was a child that time did run away with one of the men that did drive down in motorcar but after the motorcar did gone just a mile it start to heat up and plenty steam coming out of the engine and she so frighten that she jump out and run back home for she never go inside motorcar before in her whole life and she think it was going to explode. And Pa say that especially the shopkeeper them was glad because all like Mass Curly him never sell so much rum in him life and the whole heap of them get rich out of Miss Rilla misfortune.

Anyway after two weeks done Miss Rilla just appear sudden one day and give herself up to Corpie down the square. And Corpie was a Special and the most case he ever handle before is when people tief goat and is only one person, Big Head Jim, that ever tief people goat. So anytime anybody ever miss goat all Corpie do is wait till Big Head come down to Springville square and he hold him and lead him off.

So when Miss Rilla give herself up to him him never know what to do. Then him suddenly remember who she is so him rush her inside the house and shut the door and he say have some lemonade Miss Rilla and treating her like Royalty.

Then he confuse some more so he rush into the bedroom and put on him Sam Browne belt that hang on the bed post. Then he fraid she leave so he rush into the hall and when he see her sitting there so quiet he rush back inside and take off the belt and put on his blue serge pants with the blue seam at the side. Then he rush back outside to check that she still there then he run inside and put on his belt and black boots. Then he take the boots off and polish and shine them. All this time he studying that plenty trouble will cause if people find her there so he decide to hire vehicle quick and take her out of the district. So he tiptoe past Miss Rilla and put his finger to him mouth to tell her to keep quiet then he creep down to Mass Curly shop to hire car and tell Mass Curly that his wife sick and he taking her to doctor. All this time the wife over at her ground big and hearty same way but Mass Curly dont know that. So he get the car and as he drive up to the house he run inside and hustle Miss Rilla into the back seat and they take off. And when he take her to the police station they take statement from her and warn her not to run away again for she important witness in the case.

By this time news spread quick quick in Springville that she give herself up and Corpie take her gone to big police station. And every jack man woman and pickney for miles round gather in the square and they jeering and shouting and calling out and waiting for Miss Rilla to come back. And Pa who I hear all these things from say that the funny thing is that when the car finally draw up and the door open, not a living soul in the crowd move or say a word for she have a look on her face that frighten every one of them and as she get out the car they all just craning them neck and looking and holding up baby and mashing one another toe but not one make a move. Is like they all behind a invisible line and Corpie take her and lead her into his house without even thinking what he doing and he shut the door and not a soul move or say a word for about five minute afterward and everyone just move off quiet-like as if they were never there. Pa say he was there and he feel that she did get a Scienceman work a fet for her so nobody could touch her and nobody dare lift a finger against her.

And she stay in her house quiet from the day she come back till the trial and Bigger gone to Penitentiary for life and he didnt hang because it was a crime of passion Pa say and nobody ever see her come out of the house during that time though everybody watching all the time. And only Poppa D did visit her and carry food which really surprise everybody and cause plenty talking and upset because Poppa D was a big man and a decent man in the district and nobody even know that he know Miss Rilla much less and everybody say that Poppa D dont have no right mixing himself up with a scarlet woman like that even though other people say that is all the travel in foreign part make him head not so righted. But like how Poppa D did have money and was a very independent soul and people used to whisper how him connect up with the strongest Scienceman in Jamaica everybody carry on treat him with respect same way when they see him and never say a word about him or Miss Rilla to him face.

Poor poor Miss Rilla. Ai my child, poor Poppa D. I dont need all them pot with flowers at all at all. Love bloom on my doorstep, Miss Rilla used to tell me.

VI

And it was true because I never in my life see a thing like how Miss Rilla and Poppa D live nice to one another. No sir. MeMa and Pa wasnt like that at all at all. I never once see Pa bring MeMa any little sweet thing from town no matter how much goat he sell and I never see MeMa laugh the way Miss Rilla laugh soft sometime when Poppa D tease her. Sometime MeMa and Pa used to frighten me till my heart drop clear to my footbottom because, although I shouldnt be talking these things, the two of them could bruck some big fight and lick one another no fool.

Pa wasnt afraid of MeMa and she wasnt afraid of him neither because she was a big strapping woman compare to him and one time Pa did throw a vase her niece did send Ma from America and break a glass window and if you look you can see is still cardboard in the window because MeMa say she not fixing it and we all can drown when rain come and the cardboard soak and any time she mention the window and Pa is there he get mad and is another fight start again.

And another time Pa did sell some goat at May pen and when

he coming back home and reach Mass Curly shop he stop and take up a few waters and next thing we know he staggering up the road and we could hear him clear down Mister Ramsay corner the way he shouting. And from MeMa hear him she start to carry on and pray and quarrel at the same time and make plenty noise too. And what MeMa didnt know was that Pa did have him shotgun that he did leave down at Mass Curly and he just pick up the shotgun and Mass Curly sell him cheap cheap a whole heap of cartridge he did buy off a Special.

And I dont know what did vex Pa from the beginning but so he near the house so he start load the gun and so he reach up to the house so he start firing. Eh-eh! Dulcie so frighten she drop the whole pan of white clothes she was hanging out right on the ground and run a-bawl inside the house. This time MeMa so confuse she dont even notice the clothes for she calling out to the two of we to come inside and she run and shut the door and put the sofa and all the chair behind it like barricade and it was just the three of us inside the house and I frighten so till! And I did know that MeMa frighten too for I could see her face red and she sweating like mule and her tie head dropping off and she dont even notice and while she piling up the chair she saying, "Holy Father look down on your innocent little children Dulcie and Lenora your precious little lambs that dont old enough yet to bring any sin into your world and I thy servant who always serve you well and pay her tithe and see how this drunken son of a bitch is about to kill all of we and please God dont let him shoot we for I am your good and faithful servant Gretta Gayle amen."

And then she gather up the two of we and drag us into the back room and Dulcie and me so frighten we hugging one another and crying and burying our head in MeMa skirt and MeMa not paying us no mind for she too busy praying and bawling out. I tell you I never so frighten in my life for all this time Pa shooting at the house for we hear when he clip a shingle now and then but mostly he just hitting banana leaf round the house and it sounding like old cloth tearing and another time he hit the zinc roof over the tank. But I dont really think that Pa mean to shoot us for when he go bird shooting he bring home more bird than anybody else and everybody know he is the greatest bird shooter in the whole parish.

So MeMa still down on her knees praying for God to come down and rescue his poor innocent children and make tribulation and pestilence strike the drunken outside for the Lord hateth drunkenness which is a vile sin and he is an abomination in his sight (that is Pa she talking about). And is a lucky thing Pa so drunk he cant shoot straight or else I wouldnt be living to tell you this now. All this time Pa cursing like mad and making a whole heap of noise and saying how he going to kill off the whole lot of we for we is a millstone round his neck and a bunch of parasite and a lot of other things.

This time Dulcie and me still hugging one another and holding on to MeMa and she still praying loud as if she want drown out Pa and him cursing and shooting. And this go on for a long time and every time Pa get quiet we know he setting up for another shot and this take a long time and then we hear "BLAM" and bullet tear into banana leaf and this cause MeMa to pray louder as if God couldnt hear her unless she shout.

By this time we hear other people shouting at Pa but we know how these people round here stay and it sound like they all staying far away but we hear Cousin Dolphie there trying to get Pa stop shooting and go with him for another drink and Pa still cursing and shooting at the house.

Then all of a sudden it just get quiet outside and even MeMa shut up and then we hear a whole heap of people outside beating on the door and calling we to come out for Pa gone and leave the gun. So MeMa move the barricade and we go outside and we see the crowd of people and no Pa and they say he gone with Cousin Dolphie who promise him a drink. So MeMa get vex again and start curse Cousin Dolphie say is people like him leading her husband astray and causing him to spend money on rum while his children starving and cause him to do wicked deeds and make his wife a nervous wreck and a laughing stock in the district. But by this time everybody round here use to how MeMa can carry on so they dont pay her no mind and finally she quiet down and start hang out the clothes again.

Pa didnt come home till late late and he so drunk they had to carry him home and MeMa wouldnt let him in the house so they just leave him under the big mango tree with crocus bag under him head like pillow and dew fall on him and he get a bad head cold and MeMa never speak to him for one whole month and every time she hear him coughing she start sing one of her church hymn and smile a little smile and she didnt pay him no mind at all for a long time till they start talk again and quarrel again like usual.

But it wasnt only MeMa and Pa who live like that but everybody for plenty time one of MeMa church sister would come to the house with her clothes and everything and cry and say how her husband beat her and she not going to live with him again and she and MeMa lock up in the room and pray and read Bible and by the next day she would start look out of place and then she would go back to her own yard or else her husband would come and get her but you could see they not living in peace.

And is so everybody I know in the world stay, quarrel all the time. Or else two girl catch fight over man and they tear off one another clothes what a disgrace or the boys at school catch fight over marble or the big men would catch fight over woman. Lord but that is a wicked thing though . . .

Only Teacher and Teacher Wife of all the people I know did live good and never fight so I could see but they kind of starchy and not nice nice to one another like Miss Rilla and Poppa D.

Lord, Miss Rilla did love to tease Poppa D so! Like when Poppa D not working he there in the hall sitting in him underpants and merino reading Gleaner and Miss Rilla cleaning house.

She would say, "Cho Poppa D come out of my nice clean hall in yu dirty old clothes yu black and ugly sinting yu."

The first time I hear her talk like that to Poppa D my heart drop clear to my footbottom because everybody know that Poppa D quiet but he not an easy man and I expect war to bruck out right away but is only talking Miss Rilla talking for she quick and flick him with her duster cloth and he raise his head from the paper and grab her but she jump way quick time and laugh and he grab a gerbera from the vase beside him and throw at her and it dont catch her for she dance to the other side of the room and quick before she grab anything else to throw Poppa D run into the room and shut the door. And Miss Rilla knocking on the door with her two fist and laughing till she see me and she say quick time, "Hey Lenora run down to Mass Curly and get some oil for me no man".

And I take the money and I go outside but I know she dont need none for she have two big lamp full and she always doing that to me when she and Poppa D start romping as if she dont want me around and I only like to watch them for they look so happy and they make me feel happy. And sometime I stay away for days because I feel when Poppa D around Miss Rilla dont want me.

But when she see me passing she will call out "Hey little redhead gal what wrong with mi gizada eh? Cockroach inna it or you find another Miss Rilla?" and I know I happy again for I cant stay vex with Miss Rilla.

I have to tell you that Miss Rilla was like a slave driver to Poppa D sometime, the same Poppa D that so frighten everybody else. She would sit there on her rocking chair rocking and laughing and she have Poppa D out in the sunhot planting flowers for her or laying out rockstone to make flower bed. Eh-eh. And all this time she cracking joke and all the people passing hurrying by because they dont want Poppa D to see that they see him doing woman work. And Poppa D is a quiet man hardly say more than two word at a time but you can see that he dont mind at all for so he working he humming and so he work done so he come inside the house and Miss Rilla have a big pitcher of lemonade a wait for him and a big slice of pone and when he eat and drink done he put his head in her lap and she there rubbing his head and singing "Kitch" and teasing him and laughing some more. Bwoy, go see MeMa do that to Pa. Eh-eh you want fight bruck! And beside MeMa there telling us how Kitch is a dirty song and we not to sing it and she dont even like it when we hum it though how she learn that song I dont know.

And I really love to see Miss Rilla and Poppa D together for the two of them so happy and everything is nice at their house and Poppa D buy Miss Rilla plenty crockery and glasses and a pretty bedspread that she say cost whole heap of money and he also buy her a stove and a sewing machine though she cant sew and a radio just like Mass Curly own but it old now and only work sometime.

And Miss Rilla house was the prettiest house in the district though MeMa use to say how the floor never shine good. But that is not true for I use to help Miss Rilla shine her house plenty time because she have a bad heart and doctor say she not to do heavy work.

And plenty people in the district vex how Miss Rilla have all these nice things and one time she did wash her bedspread and hang it out on the front line and everybody that go past slow down to look and some even bold enough to come in and fingle the bedspread and say they admiring it and then as soon as they leave they go pass remark about how Miss Rilla extra and show-off.

And about the same time MeMa was trying to convert Big Mout Doris and was telling her how the Lord provide only for his children and make the wicked to suffer and Big Mout Doris say, "Eh, then Miss Rilla no mus be the Lawd biggest child in this district for look how she a prosper".

And MeMa did get so vex that she just shut her Bible and tell Big Mout Doris how she just say a wicked thing and was just a tough head naygah and would never find redemption she so blasphemous and fill up with evil thought.

And Big Mout Doris say, "Cho is because I talk truth and you dont like it," and MeMa say that is that she would not try with this sinner again as God is her judge. And Big Mout Doris say that alright for she never hold with no religion that say that you cant press your hair and you must wear long frock because all that happen is that them Kingston girl that does wear short frock just come down to Springville and take way all the man them. Anyway to cut long story short MeMa get vex and stop talk to Doris and the two of them keep up malice long time and is all because of Miss Rilla things.

I used to wonder if Poppa D and Miss Rilla so happy because Poppa D buy plenty pretty things for her. And I dont really know because plenty time MeMa and Pa quarrel because MeMa want Pa to buy something pretty for the house and Pa say he dont have that class of money and if she want him make blood out of stone. And MeMa vex all the time because she dont have sewing machine and radio and all them thing. And sometime again I wonder if Poppa D only buy those things for Miss Rilla because he love her and want to give her nice things.

But Miss Rilla did tell me that she only encourage Poppa D at first because he did promise to build her a pretty concrete house for the house she was living in at the time leaking bad and practically falling down over her head. She say that when he start to court her at first if he was not a man of substance in the district she wouldnt bother with him because God know Poppa D black and ugly as sin. But anyway she say that he wasnt no hothead little fly-be-night bwoy, he was an establish man and he travel to foreign and he know how to talk good and treat woman nice and bring her a whole heap of little things from town. So though at first she didnt encourage him she didnt turn him away because even though he wasnt pretty he wasnt no little nobody and he did know how to dress nice.

And he did say to her at one time: "Miss Rilla I travel all over the seven seas and is time I settle down because I want to die where I born and I want to have a son to carry on my name. But these little girls round here too flighty. I want a real woman in my yard that does know how to take care of a man. Miss Rilla I know that you are no angel but I am a man of the world for I travel and see plenty things and the foolishness that frighten the idlers round here dont frighten me. And even though you dont have the experience that travel can give a man you still understand the ways of the world Miss Rilla and the two of us have the same kind of free spirit and it dont break easy."

And Miss Rilla say that at first she did just like to hear him talk for he could talk real nice when he ready even though he wasnt a schoolmaster or parson who is the only people she ever hear talk nice so. And he did give her a pretty gold earring he bring from Panama and she still use to wear it sometime.

She say that at the time Poppa D did start courting her she was very tired of man because all they ever do is cause worries. She say that at that time in her life it was like the world of worries was down on her head.

"Lenora," she tell me, "The Lord did cast me down bad bad. O God is when yu in trouble that you really know who your friend is. Because at that time every jack man that I did think was my friend desert me not a soul to call on, not a one to talk to, them same people in the district that nowadays come fingle up my bedspread on the line. And the only friend I have in the world at the time was Poppa D. The same Poppa D you see here now. He did look after me like I was his own child and he did give me words of comfort when my heart was fit to burst from sorrow and from this heartache I did have I learn that this man is the only true friend I have in this world. And is so love bloom for me Lenora, love bloom on my doorstep just like so. Poppa D ugly like sin eh? – but he have a heart of gold and he so brave! He brave just like Daniel in the lion den for he never care at all how them ignorant people badmouthing him. No sah. Poppa D would just use them up like blotting paper if they bother him. He don't fraid of no man. So chile is fifteen year now I living with Poppa D and that man never lift a hand or give me a harsh word. A tell you child, that day Poppa D come to me in my sorrow I feel just like love light up the whole world."

VII

All the same people did have some terrible thing to say about Miss Rilla and even how when she living with Poppa D and he make her a nice house and buy her a whole set of false teeth and spend money on plenty doctor bill for her she was still a carry

ADULTERY

on her slack ways. Well I dont know because I never see it. I believe that is just because sometime Miss Rilla free and easy and happy and like to laugh and tease people plenty and everybody else round here hard and miserable and thats why they hate her so.

Take Miss Rilla and Blue Boy who used to be my friend when he was still living around here, people did even spread talk in the district about the two of them which was a scandalous lie. That Blue Boy! He was my friend because he never tease me about my red head and he used to play music so sweet that I would follow him anywhere. Blue Boy never talk much at all at all and he is the only person I know that you could walk from Springville to Charlestown with, five mile, and he wouldnt say a word for the whole time. Sometime I think he just fall dumb. Blue Boy so tall and quiet-like I love him like he was my very brother.

Miss Rilla did get to know Blue Boy through me because from I small I used to follow Blue Boy all over the place when he play the fife. And when Miss Rilla move down to Springville and I used to run down to her house and visit her if Blue Boy was passing he would stop too and sit in the shade of the jacaranda tree and play his music.

The first time he stop she run inside quick quick and put in her top plate which she didnt wear all the time because she say it burn her. And every time Blue Boy come by after that she put on pretty dress. And one time she tell Blue Boy that doctor say that she have bad heart and dont have long to live but her heart still going boops-a-boops at the same old rate and she tell Blue Boy to feel her heart how it beating strong though doctor say it bad and Blue Boy look like he confuse and like he never want to feel her heart and Miss Rilla just grab him hand and place it on her heart so he could feel it and then she pop her big laugh to let him know is only joke she running with him and so Blue Boy stop looking so serious and we all laugh.

And she would do plenty things like that and at first Blue Boy didnt understand that Miss Rilla is a jokify lady so he use to confuse but after a while he understand her better and he would start teasing her first and say, "Hi Miss Rilla how yu heart today mek me feel it going boops-a-boops," and she would make him feel her heart and the three of us would laugh.

And another time Poppa D was away drawing cane at sugar estate down in Westmoreland and Miss Rilla tell Blue Boy that she have a shelf in her bedroom that break down and she want him to fix it as Poppa D dont have time and she tell him to come inside.

And I start to follow the two of them and Miss Rilla say, "Lenora sweetheart see I put my cassava out to dry and I dont want fowl come and root it out and I also expect Mr Basil to pass today and I want to give him a message to take to town so stay there please darling and watch my cassava and flag down Mr Basil if he pass. And Lenora, if you see anybody look as if they coming in here run come and shout me first for I dont want anybody come inside the house it too untidy but with my bad heart I just cant fix it up today."

And even though I dont like stay alone I will do anything for Miss Rilla so I sit under the tree and run fowl from the cassava all day. But Mr Basil never pass in his truck and nobody pass except some little children and I tired because I dont have nobody to talk to and I dont know what taking Miss Rilla and Blue Boy in there so long and I wonder how he can fix shelf and I dont hear no hammer going.

Anyway it getting dark and MeMa will bus mi head if I stay out after dark and I cant stand it no longer so I go up to the verandah post and I call out to Miss Rilla and the house dark and I cant see a thing and Miss Rilla call out from the bedroom "I am coming darling."

She come out after a while and I notice that she not wearing her head tie which is very strange for I never see her without her head tie yet and right away I wonder if Miss Rilla and Blue Boy deceive me and in there doing it. But then I think no because it still broad daylight and everybody wait until dark to go with man except for Dorinda that go with man in canepiece in broad daylight but she dont count.

So I there feeling kind of wicked because I shouldnt be

thinking them things and then Miss Rilla say, "Come Lenora and see how Blue Boy fix up the shelf nice". And I go in the room and look and the shelf look the same to me though I never did see it when it mash down but all her little nick-nacks off the shelf and on the bed and I say yes, Blue Boy fix it nice. And then I say, "Where Blue Boy?" and she say, "Soon come," and I dont know what to say for when I go outside I see Blue Boy sitting on the back step and something tell me not to ask question and not say a word so I take the big ripe mango that Miss Rilla give me and I walk home eating the mango and trying to understand it all.

But after that day I never see Blue Boy for about a week until one evening I sitting with Miss Rilla and she very quiet and I hear Blue Boy fife coming down the hill and I think Miss Rilla hear it too for she rush inside and put in her teeth and she come back out and go on like she just hearing Blue Boy and I notice that she looking please.

But all this wasnt so long before Miss Rilla die on truck, is her bad heart kill her and so she was telling truth and that is why I take it so hard because things between us wasnt so free and easy like of old and even Blue Boy seem as if he was growing away from me.

One time I did find out that when Poppa D not there plenty time people see Blue Boy going there without me and when I ask Blue Boy about it he say, "Lenora, you just too fas' for a child your age yu know, you just love interfere in big people business".

I ask Blue Boy since when he is big people and he tell me to hush up so I cry because Blue Boy never speak to me that way before. Then he say that I not to mind is only that Miss Rilla like him to come and play some special kind of music that only she would like and when he go down there he get plenty food to eat so I not to mind. And he tell me how Miss Rilla encourage him with his music for she say he should be on Talent Show on radio he better than anybody she ever hear and she say she will lend him the money to get to Kingston.

But I still vex and say, "You was my friend first before you meet Miss Rilla and now you love she more than me".

And he say, "But Miss Rilla is your friend too".

And I say, "Yes and now the two of you is better friend to one another than you are to me".

He get vex again and start to play his fife and dont pay me no mind. And is little after that Miss Rilla die and from that night she die I dont see Blue Boy again.

VIII

Teacher used to tell me, "Lenora you interfere in people business too much and that is why you cant pay attention to your books. Why you have to know everything and ask question abut people business so? After you not Gleaner reporter".

But big people have a habit of not telling children anything and if they su-suing together as soon as you get near they stop and change the subject or else they send you down to spring for water or to shop to get something they dont need and all of it is to get rid of you. But I learn from long time that what big people talking is sweeter than any other talking and though I never used to understand plenty of what they say I learn plenty so what I do now is I dont let them see me when they talking so they cant send me away and I hide under house and listen. And that is how I come to learn so much about Miss Rilla though nobody know I know.

So this is how I come to the real sad part of the story and what happen is this.

One time Miss Rilla was living with a fellow they call Jiveman and is so they call him for he did love to do plenty jive. He did go America one time as farm worker and he come back with whole heap of dance move and clothes and bop talk and he jiving all the time.

This Jiveman did go away but he didnt like farmworking so he come back and plenty people say that he dont like any kind of working at all and he only used to catch a little work round Christmas time when he want plenty money.

So Jiveman take up to live with Miss Rilla and this was after her previous fellow Chin who was a chiney-royal did go back to him wife and children after one time Miss Rilla did burn him with a fire stick and he lick her and she get so vex she grab an axe and was going to chop him up but he run faster than she because him smaller and he also know that Miss Rilla not so easy when she vex.

Chin so frighten that he run back to his wife who was a weak little woman that would never dare raise her voice to him much less a finger. So as soon as Chin leave Jiveman go live with Miss Rilla in the house that her mother did leave her at Red Ground and people say that she did start carry on with Jiveman long before Chin did even leave but I dont know if is true for I dont born those days.

And everybody vex how Miss Rilla take up with this Jiveman because they say how he was young and all this time Miss Rilla was a hardback woman and she didnt have a good reputation for from she small she always flirting with married men. I dont know if is true but I hear Big Mout Doris say that plenty of the girls in the district did vex because Jiveman was so handsome and did dress so well and could dance so good and the whole lot of them was after him when he take up with Miss Rilla.

Jiveman was a real sweetman because he didnt work and all the time he down Mass Curly shop playing domino and dancing and giving out him jive talk. Some people say when he drunk he have a mean temper and other people say that he didnt have to have even one drink to mean. And he quick quick to pull knife on anybody who bother him. One time after he drink plenty whites he get rough and nearly mash up the whole of Mass Curly shop and is only because Miss Rilla offer to pay for damages that they dont prison him. And everybody say how Miss Rilla just forming fool of herself over young boy.

This Jiveman live with Miss Rilla for about two year and Miss Rilla is the one who have to sell coffee and chocolate to make money to buy things for them. But all the while he there wearing pretty ganzie and serge pants and shiny shiny boot and him just walking the road all day rolling dice in him pocket or waiting for evening come to lick domino.

So now there was another man living in the district name Bigger. Bigger used to help Pa in him ground and MeMa always did say that Bigger did help Pa build the very house we living in with his own two hand and how Bigger was a good Christian boy and couldnt hurt cockroach and didnt drink and play domino like that other worthless lot that hang out at Mass Curly shop piazza and is only because he get into the clutches of that Jezebel that he come down and fall into the Pit of Sin.

MeMa always say, "the laws of man is a one eye law for the innocent is made to punish while the wicked go scot free as God is me judge that woman walking about on government good road breathing God free air without shame is the biggest criminal in the whole wide world and she should be behind bars instead of Bigger and Bigger should be out here free as a bird".

"God is a just God," MeMa always saying, "And what man foul up on this earth God will set right when the Great Revival come again or if not when God himself come back down to the wicked earth to judge both the quick and the dead, the fast and the slow. And when the trumpet sound Bigger poor boy who has suffered all these years will be redeemed and asked to take his rightful place in the Heavenly Host after God has purified him of his sins and that Rilla and Jiveman will burn in God fire everlasting".

This was MeMa favourite saying and everytime the subject come up she let forth with these words.

But the thing is that until this thing happen that day not a soul did even know that Bigger was fooling round Miss Rilla though how it is possible in this district for people even to cough without the whole world hear I dont know.

The thing was that everybody did have Bigger like little boy round the place and not paying him no serious mind for they all believe that he such a quiet decent fellow that he could never get into no trouble.

He used to live near Miss Rilla and sometimes he would stop

to chop wood for her and run to shop and so forth and nobody ever suspect anything at all between them so nobody know how long anything going on. All the same everybody did know that Jiveman didnt like Bigger and Bigger take care to stay away from Jiveman but they all say that Jiveman have red eye and worthless and that is why he dont like Bigger who is a clean living Christian boy.

So that year everybody did get a little Christmas work from Government to widen the road. To tell you the truth if is like Christmas work these days is more joking and laughing than working for they used to sing some song as they go along and the woman would cook some big pot of food under the nearest tree and when sun get too hot everybody break for more eating and joking.

Bigger and Jiveman was both working on the road gang and everytime Bigger come near Jiveman would get mean though Bigger never say anything. And every day Jiveman would pass word for Bigger and every day Bigger would just cut him eye and say nothing. So everything go on like that until one day when Jiveman and Miss Rilla must be have quarrel for Jiveman come to work and he not jiving at all he there looking meaner than ever.

Next thing everybody know Miss Rilla coming fast down the road and her face look like hell to pay and she cursing Jiveman all the way. So right away everybody stop work to watch the spree. And Miss Rilla cursing Jiveman how he worthless for he take some money that she did hide under her mattress and Jiveman cursing her all kind of name and big kas-kas going on between them. In the middle of the argument, Jiveman must be say something bout how it better him take the money than she give it to her sweetman Bigger.

Bigger? See here, everybody nearly drop dead.

So everybody turn to look at Bigger and he standing there not saying one word so nobody know if they should believe it or not till Miss Rilla say, "Yes, better give it to Bigger for he better man than you".

See here Lord! Jiveman turn wild same time and jump on

132

Bigger and start wave him finger in Bigger face. Next thing everybody know Bigger no turn bad and start trace Jiveman good as he getting. By this time everybody start get frighten and dont know what to do and Jiveman suddenly push Bigger.

Well, nobody who was there that day can give a full account of what happen next for all they see is Bigger come up fast with a machete flashing in his hand, flashing and flashing at Jiveman. The women start scream and the men they try to get at Bigger but is like the boy gone mad for he slashing away at Jiveman even after he drop to the ground and the blood just flowing away from him into the sunhot. O God. Never before such a thing happen in this district.

Everybody fall into confusion and one of the boys run to call Corpie. By the time Corpie run up there they finally cool down Bigger and someone tie him up with a rope and when they examine Jiveman he dead in truth.

And Pa say that Bigger just stand there with the rope round him not moving or saying no word like he struck dumb and so he stay till they finally get one Black Maria come from May Pen and the police take him away. And that is when everybody get over the shock and they move Jiveman and throw water over the road to wash away the blood and nobody can find Miss Rilla all somebody remember is that as Bigger kill Jiveman she running and running up the road by herself, all alone.

Well, that was a time of great sadness and confusion for everybody did like Bigger and while the trial last practically everybody from Red Ground and Springville travel to court-house to watch the whole thing or give evidence. And they didnt send Bigger to hang but they give him life and hard labour. And when they hear the sentence the women bawl out in courthouse and they had was to carry Miss Rilla away under police escort for they ready to tear her limb from limb. And that is why MeMa hate Miss Rilla so and never cry at her funeral. Poor Miss Rilla.

I dont understand about murder and things like that and when they talk is so long ago that is not like the Miss Rilla I really know. And I dont see why people have to suffer for sin all

133

turn away from SIN, change, undo

their life but is so MeMa say. There is no forgiveness without
repentance and Miss Rilla die so quick on truck I sure she never
have time to talk to no God. And if there is no forgiveness it
mean that Miss Rilla is down there burning in hell fire. But I
tell you already that I dont believe that at all, I believe that
Miss Rilla laughing so much that Saint Peter take her in just to
brighten up Heaven.

And I tell you sometime when MeMa go on so and Teacher
there nagging me and all the verb and things mix up in my head
I feel I cant go through with it. I dont care if I dont turn teacher
with press hair and new dress. I believe it better to be someone
that can laugh and make other people laugh and be happy too.
And sometime I get down on my knee and pray for the Lord to
come and take me so I can see for myself where Miss Rilla gone
to.

repent -
turn away from SIN
dedicate oneself to
         the amendment of one's life

The Jumbie Bird

Ismith Khan

The tragic story of an East Indian family stranded in Trinidad, betrayed by the authorities and discarded by Mother India.

No-one can escape the sinister call of the Jumbie bird, a ghostly message of death. It haunts the childhood world of Jamini: his fierce, proud grandfather, Kale Khan, a born fighter who dreams of returning to India; his father, a struggling jeweller; and the doomed relationship with his childhood sweetheart, Lakshmi.

The Jumbie bird returns, a symbolic and fearful omen, as Kale Khan prepares for his final battle.

'A new and exciting voice . . .
exotic and baroque . . .
moves with its own poetry'
Caribbean Quarterly

Longman Caribbean Writers Series

ISBN 0 582 78619 3

Listen, the Wind
and other stories

Roger Mais
edited by Ken Ramchand

An important selection of short stories by one of Jamaica's greatest writers, Roger Mais (author of *Brother Man, The Hills were Joyful Together* and *Black Lightning*). The collection has been edited by one of the Caribbean's leading scholars, Kenneth Ramchand, professor of English at the University of the West Indies, Trinidad. It includes work that has never previously been published, as well as many of Mais's best-known stories.

Longman Caribbean Writers Series

ISBN 0 582 78551 0

Plays for Today

Edited by Errol Hill

Three outstanding plays by three of the Caribbean's greatest playwrights brought together for the first time in one volume.

Ti-Jean and his Brothers was Derek Walcott's first venture into musical plays and is still his most popular work. A lilting St Lucian folk-tale, it tells the story of a poor family who dwell on the edge of a magical forest haunted by the devil's spirits. The brilliance of Walcott's writing draws us into the realms of fantasy where the actual and the miraculous collide.

Dennis Scott's *An Echo in the Bone* is set during a traditional Nine-Night Ceremony held to honour the spirit of the dead. Shattering sequential time in a series of dreamlike episodes the play takes us back to the time of plantations and slavery — and the savage murder of the white estate owner. Who killed Mr Charles? The answers lie deep in the racial memory, they 'echo in the bone'.

The giddy atmosphere of carnival is the setting for Errol Hill's *Man Better Man*, a rumbustuous, colourful comedy musical about stickfighters. With dance and song the battling troubadours and the calypsonian weave a tale of bravery, superstition and fraudulence. When first performed the *Times* described it as 'a blazing electrifying feast of rhythm and colour'.

Longman Caribbean Writers Series

ISBN 0 582 78620 7